PETER

Ideas A to Z Series

26 Fun-filled Learning Activities on Bible Characters

PETER

Phyllis Vos Wezeman, Anna L. Liechty, and Judith Harris Chase

kregel
PUBLICATIONS

Grand Rapids, MI 49501

Ideas A–Z Series: Peter by Phyllis Vos Wezeman, Anna L. Liechty, and Judith Harris Chase

© 1998 by Kregel Publications

Published by Kregel Publications, a division of Kregel, Inc., P.O. Box 2607, Grand Rapids, MI 49501. Kregel Publications provides trusted, biblical publications for Christian growth and service. Your comments and suggestions are valued.

Cover illustration: Patrick Kelley
Cover design: Alan G. Hartman
Book design: Nicholas G. Richardson

Library of Congress Cataloging-in-Publication Data
Wezeman, Phyllis Vos.
    Peter / Phyllis Vos Wezeman, Anna L. Liechty, Judith Harris Chase.
        p.   cm.   (Ideas A to Z series; 4)
    Includes bibliographical references.
    1. Peter, the Apostle, Saint—Study and teaching (Elementary). 2. Bible—N.T.—Study and teaching. 3. Christian education of children. I. Liechty, Anna L. II. Chase, Judith Harris. III. Title. IV. Series.
BS2515.W465   1998   225.9'2—dc21   97-38010
                                                                                    CIP

ISBN 0-8254-3962-0

Printed in the United States of America
1 2 3/04 03 02 01 00 99 98

CONTENTS

INTRODUCTION

Taking a look at the shelves in Christian bookstores, one can almost come to a conclusion that writers of religious education books have taken too literally God's command to be fruitful and multiply! With the deluge of available materials, why on earth do we offer the *Ideas A–Z* series?

First of all, *Ideas A–Z* provides an in-depth look at Scripture, at both the people and the important themes. Using twenty-six different viewpoints assures readers of thoughtful and thorough reflections on Bible topics. Each perspective provides opportunities for experiencing the lesson on a variety of levels, allowing readers and participants to discover the story in a way appropriate to their stages in life and faith development.

Ideas A–Z also develops a unique format for delivering insights, information, and activities. The A–Z topics offer a balanced variety of methods and approaches for experiencing the Bible story. For every letter of the alphabet there is a different theme and a different way of exploring that theme, like puppetry, music, drama, games, or storytelling. Such experiential learning also takes into consideration the needs of all learning styles.

Another aspect of the format is its flexibility. Each idea, A–Z, can be used alone or combined with ideas from other letters to develop a lesson plan, a worship experience, or an intergenerational activity. The ideas can simply be used to supplement existing curricula, or they can be referred to like a handbook. The format is user-friendly and open-ended, providing essential information yet fostering creative applications.

From beginning students of the Bible to more advanced learners, *Ideas A–Z* can inspire and motivate participants to keep looking at the Scriptures in fresh ways and keep applying the Bible's principles to their own lives.

So although Peter's story has been told, retold, written about, and rewritten countless times, *Ideas A–Z* offers today's descendants of Peter an opportunity to explore and experience the adventure from beginning to end, from A to Z. This experience will encourage us as we learn from Peter what it takes to be a follower of Christ.

OVERVIEW

WHO?

Who was Simon Peter? The answer's as easy as one, two, three! Simon was one of the first twelve men called to be a follower of Jesus. First to be recorded in the biblical lists of the disciples, Simon Peter was the leader and spokesperson for the group. Notably, Simon was the first disciple to acknowledge Jesus as the Son of God—the Messiah—and the first apostle to proclaim the Good News of salvation to both the Jews and the Gentiles.

Simon Peter was a person with two names. His Hebrew name, Symeon, was probably changed to Simon, a Greek name of similar sound. Peter was the descriptive name Jesus conferred on him after his confession of faith recorded in Matthew 16:16. In Aramaic the word Jesus used is *Kepha,* which means stone or rock. Using Greek letters to transliterate the Aramaic it comes out *Cephas,* which translated into Greek is *Petros,* or Peter.

Peter was originally a fisherman of Bethsaida and Capernaum, and even his occupation had two natures. When he left the sea to follow the Savior, his mission changed from catching shoals of fish to challenging souls to faith.

Simon Peter was a person with three opportunities. During Jesus' trial, Peter was given three occasions to identify with the Christ, yet Peter denied Jesus each time. After the Resurrection Jesus offered Peter three opportunities for restoration when He asked "Do you love me?" Jesus recommissioned Peter by responding to Peter's affirmative answers with three challenges to "Feed the flock."

Empowered by the Holy Spirit—the third person of the Trinity—on the day of Pentecost, Peter preached the story of Jesus' life, death, and resurrection and three thousand people believed and were baptized. Peter became a leader of the early Christian church, spreading the Good News to the Jews and to the Gentiles.

Who was Simon Peter? One man with two names empowered by the Holy Spirit to spread God's message of the salvation Jesus offers to all people.

WHAT?

Simon, the brother of Andrew and the son of John, was a native of Bethsaida and a fisherman called to be one of Jesus' first twelve disciples. During the course of Peter's participation in Jesus' earthly ministry, several significant events occurred. Peter confessed Jesus to be the Messiah, the Son of God, in response to Jesus' question "Who do men say that I am?" Based on this profession, Jesus conferred the name Peter—or rock—on his follower because Peter's statement of faith formed the foundation for the creeds and confessions of the Christian church. Simon Peter was present at the Transfiguration, he denied Jesus three times during the trial, and was an eyewitness to the Easter event. Following the Resurrection, Peter was forgiven by Jesus and commissioned to shepherd His flock.

After Jesus' ascension, Peter became the leader of the group gathered at Jerusalem. Empowered by the Holy Spirit, Peter preached a sermon on Pentecost and three thousand people were converted and baptized. During his later ministry, Peter performed several miracles; led Cornelius, the centurion, to Christ; was arrested and imprisoned for spreading the Gospel; and conducted several missionary journeys.

In his later life, Peter wrote two of the New Testament letters, 1 and 2 Peter, and probably provided first-hand accounts of Jesus' ministry for Mark's gospel. It is reported that Peter died in Rome during the persecutions that took place under Emperor Nero. Tradition says that he was crucified on an upside-down cross because he did not feel worthy to die in the same manner as Jesus.

WHEN?

Timeline

A timeline provides a way to put the events of history in order—to actually visualize what happened at what point in time. Because the Christian world uses the birth of Jesus to divide and date history, abbreviations in a timeline often include B.C., B.C.E., and A.D. B.C. stands for before Christ, B.C.E. refers to before the common era or before the Christian era, and A.D., for the Latin words *Anno Domini*, mean "in the year of our Lord." The letter c., an abbreviation for circa, before a date means around or about that year. It is important to note that dates vary depending on the reference material used to compile a timeline. Use the timeline provided as a guide for putting biblical events into perspective, but refer to additional resources to supplement the information.

Undated	Creation
Undated	Adam and Eve; the Fall; Cain and Abel
Undated	Noah; the Flood
Undated	Tower of Babel
2100 B.C.	Abraham
2066 B.C.	Abraham and Isaac
2006 B.C.	Jacob and Esau
1900 B.C.	Joseph in Egypt
1700–1250 B.C.	Hebrews in Egypt
1526 B.C.	Moses born
1450 B.C.	the Exodus; Moses and the Law
1399 B.C.	Joshua; the Promised Land
1375 B.C.	judges begin to rule Israel
1209 B.C.	Deborah
1162 B.C.	Gideon
1105 B.C.	Samuel born
1070 B.C.	Samson
1050 B.C.	Saul becomes Israel's first king
1000–961 B.C.	David reigns as king
970 B.C.	Solomon becomes king
959 B.C.	the temple in Jerusalem completed
930 B.C.	the kingdom of Israel divides
875 B.C.	Elijah and the prophets
793 B.C.	Jonah
740 B.C.	Isaiah
605 B.C.	Daniel
586 B.C.	Jerusalem and the temple destroyed
537 B.C.	first Jewish exiles return from captivity
516 B.C.	new temple completed in Jerusalem
479 B.C.	Mordecai, Esther, and Haman
445 B.C.	Nehemiah builds Jerusalem wall
333 B.C.	Judea made part of Greek empire
63 B.C.	Rome occupies Judea
40–4 B.C.	Herod the Great, king of Judea
7–4 B.C.	Jesus born

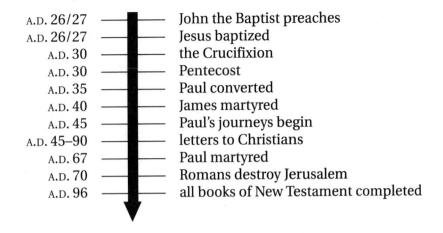

A.D. 26/27	John the Baptist preaches
A.D. 26/27	Jesus baptized
A.D. 30	the Crucifixion
A.D. 30	Pentecost
A.D. 35	Paul converted
A.D. 40	James martyred
A.D. 45	Paul's journeys begin
A.D. 45–90	letters to Christians
A.D. 67	Paul martyred
A.D. 70	Romans destroy Jerusalem
A.D. 96	all books of New Testament completed

WHERE?

Scripture Passages

One hundred and fifty to two hundred references to the life and ministry of Peter are recorded in the Bible, especially in Matthew, Mark, Luke, John, and Acts. Peter is mentioned in the Epistles—especially Galatians—and he is credited with writing 1 and 2 Peter. Refer to a concordance for a complete list of passages pertaining to Peter.

Highlights of Peter's life are contained in the following Scripture selections:

- Call of Simon (Matthew 4:18–22; Mark 1:16–20; Luke 5:1–11)
- Call and renaming of Simon (John 1:35–42)
- Healing of Simon's mother-in-law (Matthew 8:14–17; Mark 1:29–31; Luke 4:38–41)
- Peter walks on the sea (Matthew 14:22–32)
- Peter's confession (Matthew 16:13–20; Mark 8:27–30; Luke 9:18–22)
- Peter and the Transfiguration (Matthew 17:1–8; Mark 9:2–8; Luke 9:28–36; 2 Peter 1:16–21)
- Peter and feet washing (John 13:1–11)
- Bold promises and Gethsemane (Matthew 26:30–46; Mark 14:26–42; Luke 22:31–34, 39–53)
- Peter and the sword (Matthew 26:51–54; Luke 22:47–53; John 18:10–11)
- Peter's denial (Matthew 26:69–75; Mark 14:66–72; Luke 22:54–62; John 18:15–27)
- Peter and Easter (Mark 16:7; Luke 24:34; John 20:2–10; 1 Corinthians 15:4–5)
- Forgiveness and commissioning (John 21:1–22)
- Peter takes the lead (Acts 1:15ff.; 5:1–11)
- Peter's preaching (Acts 2:13–42; 3:11–26)
- Peter's healing powers (Acts 3:1–10; 9:36–43)
- Peter's boldness in face of arrests (Acts 4:1–31; 5:12–42)
- Peter's vision and response (Acts 10:1–48; 11:1–18)
- Peter's arrest and release (Acts 12:1–19)
- Peter at council of Jerusalem (Acts 15)
- Peter as seen by Paul (Galatians 1:11–24; 1:24–2:21; 1 Corinthians 1:12; 3:22; 9:5; 15:5)
- Peter from Rome (1 Peter 5:13; 2 Peter)

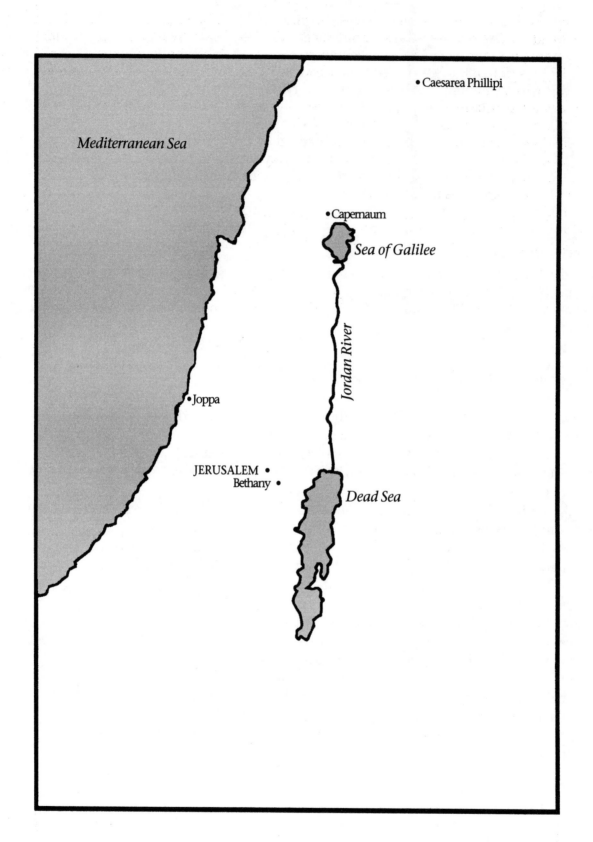

Mediterranean Sea

• Caesarea Phillipi

• Capernaum

Sea of Galilee

Jordan River

•Joppa

JERUSALEM •
Bethany •

Dead Sea

WHY?

Peter is one of the most interesting people we meet in the New Testament. He is a study in contrasts. On the one hand, he is a recognized leader among the disciples. Jesus frequently singles him out to be a special companion and recognizes his leadership, thus elevating him from a fisherman to a leader of the church. Peter is also first in line to confess that Jesus is the Christ, the Son of God. On the other hand, Peter is first to deny his Lord.

Peter has humble beginnings and significant character defects, yet Jesus makes him a leader. While studying Peter is interesting in itself, what we read in the Scriptures about Peter tells us even more about Jesus. It reveals to us the depth of His forgiving love. As Jesus is facing death and suffering greatly, we see Him forgiving Peter who was so quick to deny Jesus in order to save himself. If Jesus can forgive Peter's denial in His moment of greatest need, the message is clear: He can forgive us as well.

Furthermore, Jesus takes this impetuous, character-flawed fisherman and makes him a leader of His people. He not only forgives Peter, but uses him, character defects and all, to build a new creation. The apostle Paul writes about all things becoming new in Christ Jesus. Peter was certainly an example of this—and his example offers hope for us as well. We, too, can become new creatures in Christ Jesus.

PETER: *Ideas A–Z Series*

A

APOSTLE

Purpose
To learn how God used Peter as a "sent one" and how God can use each of us as an apostle of the faith.

Preparation
- Spiral notebook and pencil/pen
- Portable cassette tape recorder
- Video camera (if available)
- Videotape player and television

Advance Preparation
- Use a Bible concordance to find verses in the New Testament that relate incidents in Peter's life. List prominent passages in their biblical order.
- Plan a time (after a church service, at a nursing home, etc.) to conduct interviews.

Procedure
Our English word *apostle* is a transliteration of the Greek word *apostolos*, taken from the verb which means "to send." It is a term that carries with it the sense of being commissioned. Authority is given to and responsibility is placed upon the one sent. A short definition of an apostle, therefore, is "one sent on a definite mission with full authority on behalf of the sender and is accountable to the him" ("Apostle," *Evangelical Dictionary of Theology,* ed. Walter A. Elwell [Grand Rapids: Baker, 1984], 70). While the term *apostle* traditionally is applied to a limited number of people (the first disciples, Paul, and James), in a generic sense it applies to all Christians who have been sent by Jesus to take the Good News to everyone.

Divide the group into teams of three or four participants each. Assign each team the mission of interviewing three or more adults and asking the following questions:

- What was your first job?
- What person taught you the most about that job?
- Have you ever changed careers or had to learn a new job? Why?
- How did you learn a new career or job?
- What do you like best about your present occupation?

If possible, have each team use a video camera to record their interview (an adult or teen may need to serve as camera operator). A battery-operated cassette tape recorder can be used in place of a video camera. If recording equipment is not available, have the team record answers in a notebook.

After each team has conducted their interviews, review them as a group. Note particularly people who have made career changes and the reasons for their choices.

Have the whole group review the Bible verses on the life of Peter and note how Jesus changed Peter's occupation from fishing for fish to fishing for people. Then have the group answer the following questions:

- What motivated Peter to leave his fishing business and follow Jesus?
- What specific mission did Peter fulfill as an apostle?
- What specific mission does God have for each of us as Christians?

B

BETRAYAL

Purpose
To review the biblical account of Peter's betrayal of Jesus and Jesus' forgiveness of Peter and to make and use puppets to tell a modern-day story of betrayal and forgiveness.

Preparation
- Paper or Styrofoam plates
- Styrofoam trays
- Markers
- Construction paper
- Glue
- Paint stirrers
- Duct tape
- Fabric, plastic bags, or tissue paper
- "Timothy Turtle's Terrible Temptation" script

Procedure
Matthew 26:69–75; Mark 14:66–72; Luke 22:54–65; and John 18:25–27 record the account of Peter's betrayal of Jesus. After His arrest Jesus was taken to Caiaphas, the high priest, for questioning. While Peter waited in the courtyard, three different people approached him and asked if he was one of Jesus' followers. Each time Peter replied that he did not know the man. Peter betrayed Jesus by denying that he was one of Jesus' disciples. Fortunately, the story doesn't end there. John 21:15–19 contains the report of a meeting between Peter and Jesus after the Resurrection. Just as Peter had denied, or betrayed, Jesus three times, Jesus offers Peter three opportunities to be forgiven. Three times Jesus asks Peter if he loves Him. When Peter answers "Yes!" Jesus commissions the disciple—the student—to become an apostle—one who tells others that Jesus is the Savior, the only One who can offer true and lasting forgiveness. Once Peter realizes that he is forgiven, he is empowered to carry the message of salvation to the world.

"Timothy Turtle's Terrible Temptation" is also a story about betrayal and forgiveness. Timothy Turtle, the main character, sticks his neck out and tells a secret to Dotty Duck. When Timothy discovers that Dotty has betrayed the confidence to Herman Hound, he goes into his shell and is tempted to be unforgiving. However, Timothy soon realizes that he cannot get anywhere in life this way. Leo Lion finally convinces Timothy to come out of his shell and to experience the freedom of forgiveness.

This story, in puppet show format, teaches the important truth that being unforgiving and harboring resentment ultimately diminishes the person who is unforgiving and resentful even more than the person who caused the initial injury. Being unforgiving cuts one off from reconciliation and love as well as from further injury.

There is also, however, another theme to the story. Timothy learns that loving relationships require taking risks. People who care about each other sometimes hurt one another. Sometimes this happens by accident and other times it happens in a moment of anger or vindictiveness. Regardless of the reason for the hurt, all close relationships involve some pain. Timothy learns that loving and being loved requires risking, and sometimes enduring, hurt and pain. The care and love that friends share with each other is something to be cherished and nourished in spite of the pain we may also have to endure.

Use "Timothy Turtle's Terrible Temptation" to help participants realize that everyone is in need of forgiveness—every day! Make paper plate puppets to represent Timothy Turtle, Dotty Duck, Herman Hound, and Leo Lion. Wash Styrofoam plates and meat and produce trays and use them for the project too.

With marker or construction paper scraps, form a face on one side of the plate. Add hair made from these and other materials. Glue the pieces in place.

Tape or glue a paint stirrer, craft stick, or dowel rod to the back of the plate to use as the handle by which the puppet is operated.

Fabric pieces, plastic bags, or tissue paper can be added to the rod to create a costume.

TIMOTHY TURTLE'S TERRIBLE TEMPTATION SCRIPT

SCENE I: Timothy tells Dotty a secret.

DOTTY

[Enters and plays or sings]

TIMOTHY

[Enters]

DOTTY

Hi, Timothy. How come you're so late? School has been out for 45 minutes.

TIM

Well, would you believe that I'm just slower than you?

DOTTY

Of course you're slower, you're a turtle, but you usually don't take this long to get home from school.

TIM

It's such a beautiful day, I just took my time.

DOTTY

Come on, it's been cloudy all day and it looks like it will rain any minute. I don't think you're telling me the whole story.

TIM

Well, I guess I can trust you. I just don't want my parents to find out. I'll tell you if you promise you won't tell anyone else.

DOTTY

Sure, you can tell me. I can keep a secret.

TIM

I don't want to ruffle your feathers, but you have to promise.

DOTTY

OK, I promise.

TIM

Well, I'm really sticking my neck out, but since you promised I guess I can trust you. I failed my math test. Mrs. Badger made me stay after school and do some practice problems and then take the test over.

DOTTY

What's so bad about that?

TIM

Well, my parents told me that if I didn't get a good grade on my math test that I'd be in hot water.

DOTTY

You don't have to worry about me, I won't tell a soul.

TIM

I'd better hurry home before I'm in even more trouble.

[Dotty and Timothy exit]

SCENE II: Dotty Duck tells Herman Hound the secret.

HERMAN

[Enters]

DOTTY

[Enters]

Hi, Herman, can you pause awhile or do you have to be running along.

HERMAN

I can stay awhile. What's cooking?

DOTTY

Timothy's going to be if his parents . . . *[slight pause]*. Oh, oh, I can't tell you about it. I promised.

HERMAN

Tell me what? I'll just hound you until you do.

DOTTY

I really shouldn't. Tim said that his parents would have him in hot water if they found out. I wouldn't want Tim to get steamed with me.

HERMAN

I'm not going to tell his parents. It's OK.

DOTTY

Well, I guess it wouldn't hurt to tell you.

HERMAN

Good, I'm all ears.

DOTTY

Well, Timothy failed his math test. Mrs. Badger made him stay after school to practice his math and then take the test again. You know how slow Timothy is. It took him 45 minutes to get here. His parents told him that he'd be in hot water if he didn't get a good grade on the test.

HERMAN

Wow! I wonder what he's going to tell his parents.

DOTTY

I don't know. Be sure you don't tell anybody. I wouldn't want them to find out. Timothy would probably never forgive me if they did.

HERMAN

Don't worry, why would I tell anyone? Besides, no one would tell his folks.

[Dotty and Herman both exit]

SCENE III: Leo talks to Timothy.

TIMOTHY

[Already on stage, head pulled in]

LEO

[Enters, sees Tim; Loudly, looking into shell . . .]

Timothy, are you in there? *[Pause]* Tim, are you in there? *[Pause]* Tim, gonna come out?

TIM

[Muffled] Go away. I don't ever want to talk to anybody again.

LEO

Tim, it's just me, your friend Leo.

TIM

[Muffled] It was a friend who got me in trouble.

LEO

I didn't hurt you, did I?

TIM

[Muffled] No, it was Dotty. I told her a secret and asked her not to tell anyone. She even promised. But my parents found out and I got in deep trouble. I'm never going to trust anyone again, and I'm not ever going to forgive Dotty for what she did.

LEO

You must really have felt hurt, but I thought that you were more thick-skinned than that.

TIM

I knew I was sticking my neck out when I did it, but I thought I could trust her. Now I'm never going to stick my neck out again.

LEO

That's pretty heavy stuff to carry around with you. I do wonder one thing, though.

TIM

What's that?

LEO

How are you ever going to get anywhere in life if you stay in your shell like this?

TIM

What do you mean?

LEO

Well, if you keep your head inside you can't get anywhere because you can't see where you're going.

TIM

Well . . .

LEO

Besides, if you forgive Dotty you will get a tremendous load off your back.

TIM

But I don't want to get hurt again either.

LEO

Nobody wants to get hurt by their friends, but if we just pull inside and hide we can't enjoy them either.

TIM

[*Tentatively sticking head out*] Well, I guess so. I don't want to get hurt, but I guess it would get pretty lonely in here all by myself.

LEO

We all get hurt by friends, but if we don't forgive them we really hurt ourselves even more. We make ourselves lonely and unhappy.

TIM

[*Sticking head out all the way*] Yeah, I guess you're right, Leo.

LEO

What are you going to say to Dotty the next time you see her?

TIM

[*Both exiting*] That's a good question.

SCENE IV: Timothy and Dotty meet again.

DOTTY

[*Enters and looks around*]

TIM

[*Enters*]

Hello, Dotty.

DOTTY

[*Hesitantly*] Uh . . ., hi, Timothy. Uh . . . how are you?

TIM

Well, I got into a lot of trouble over my math test, but I guess that's all over now. Other than that I'm OK.

DOTTY

I'm sorry, Tim. I guess it was kind of my fault that you got in trouble. I told Herman about the test after I promised you I'd keep your secret.

TIM

That's all right, Dotty. I've forgiven you. Once I forgave you it felt like a big weight had been lifted off of me.

DOTTY

I'm relieved too. I was afraid that you wouldn't ever forgive me.

TIM

I was tempted to crawl into my shell for a while, but Leo convinced me that I'd never get anywhere in life like that and that I'd be pretty lonely without any friends.

DOTTY

Great. Let's go for a swim.

TIM

OK, suits me!

CONFESSION

Purpose
To write a "Scripture Script" and to dramatize Peter's confession that Jesus is the Messiah.

Preparation
- Bibles
- Paper
- Pencils or pens
- Scripture script outline
- Sample script
- Costume pieces (optional)

Procedure
"Jesus is the Messiah, the Son of God!" (Matthew 16:16; Mark 8:29; Luke 9:20). Peter's response to Jesus' question, "Who do people say that I am?" is an affirmation that forms the basis for the historic creeds and confessions of the Christian church. Peter's confession of faith is important because it reveals the true identity of Jesus—Christ the Savior, the Son of God. "Who do you say that I am?" is a question that each believer must still answer today. All believers, in all times and places, are joined to the church by faith in Jesus Christ as Savior, the same faith that Peter expressed in Bible times.

Help the students experience the story of Peter's confession through the use of drama. Learn a process called "Characterization of a Bible Passage" and create an easy script from the words of Matthew 16:13–20 by following four simple steps. The goal is to arrange the Bible verses into character parts so that the passage will be more understandable to those who hear it. The object is not to embellish the text nor add details that are not suggested, but to adhere as closely as possible to the words of the Bible.

——— SCRIPTURE SCRIPT OUTLINE ———

Step One
Identify the characters in the passage and make a list of these people.

Step Two
Find all of the quotes in the passage. Match a character to each of them. Write the person's name on the left side of a paper, and write the words of the quote next to it. Try to break long passages into several parts.

Step Three
Write lines for any portion of the passage that could be assigned to a specific person. Clues to look for are words or phrases that suggest that the narrative could be written in dialogue form.

Step Four
Add a narrator, or several, to provide information between the speaking parts.

A sample script, based on Matthew 16:13–20, is provided. The words are taken from the New International Version of the Bible. Use this script, or one written by the teacher or students, to review the story of Peter's confession.

Take turns having the students play the parts: narrator, Jesus, Peter, and the disciples. Combine or expand the disciple's parts based on the numbers of people in the group. As an option, drape strips of fabric over the actors' heads and shoulders to create simple costumes.

At the conclusion of the drama, gather the group in a circle. Invite each person to reflect silently on Jesus' question, "Who do you say that I am?" Remind the students that faith is a very personal matter. No one—parent, teacher, or friend—can make a decision of faith for another person. Each person must answer for him- or herself. Offer a prayer that each student will personally come to know Jesus as God's Son, the Messiah.

—— SAMPLE SCRIPT ——

NARRATOR
When Jesus came to the region of Caesarea Philippi, he asked his disciples a question.

JESUS
Who do people say that the Son of Man is?

DISCIPLE ONE
John the Baptist

DISCIPLE TWO
Elijah

DISCIPLE THREE
Jeremiah

DISCIPLE FOUR
One of the prophets

JESUS
But who do you say that I am?

PETER
You are the Christ, the Son of the living God.

JESUS
Blessed are you, Simon son of Jonah! For this was not revealed to you by man, but my Father in heaven.

DISCIPLE ONE
Jesus continued.

JESUS
You are Peter, and on this rock I will build my church, and the gates of Hades will not overcome it.

DISCIPLE TWO
Jesus had more to say to Peter.

JESUS
I will give you the keys of the kingdom of heaven, and whatever you bind on earth will be bound in heaven, and whatever you loose on earth will be loosed in heaven.

DISCIPLE THREE
Then Jesus ordered us not to tell anyone that He was the Christ.

D

DISCIPLES

Purpose
To define the word *disciple* and to use riddles to review information about the first disciples.[1]

Preparation
- Riddle Sheets
- Duplicating equipment
- Paper
- Bibles
- Bible storybooks
- Pencils or pens

Advance Preparation
- Duplicate a Riddle Sheet for each participant.

Procedure
Many terms can be used to define the word *disciple:* adherent, apostle, believer, convert, devotee, follower, learner, listener, pupil, student, witness. Basically, a disciple is a pupil or follower of a teacher or school. In this case, the word *disciple* refers to an early follower of Jesus, especially any of the original twelve and the one replacement, later called the apostles, and to a follower of Jesus—past, present, and future—known by the term *Christian.*

Peter was one of the first disciples—the twelve people Jesus called to follow Him in a special way. Other disciples included Andrew, James, John, Philip, Bartholomew, Matthew, Thomas, James the Less, Jude/Thaddaeus, Simon the Zealot, Judas Iscariot, and Matthias, the replacement for Judas Iscariot.

Because the selection of the twelve disciples was such an important consideration, Jesus spent the entire night praying to His Father before He came to His decision (Luke 6:12–13). These twelve people would be chosen, called, taught, and commissioned to be the messianic community, first to the "lost sheep of Israel," and then to the world at large. They would be the ones responsible for carrying on Jesus' ministry after He was no longer on earth. Jesus' call to His first special group of followers not only changed their lives and the lives of their families and friends, it changed our lives as well. Though the commission to go into all the world to preach the Gospel and to baptize believers (Matthew 28:18–20) was entrusted to the twelve men Jesus called during Bible times, it has been passed on through the ages and is ours today. Since Jesus has chosen each of us who are His followers as His modern day disciples, we can learn much from the first disciples of Jesus, using them as our example for the work we are to do in today's world.

Review information about Jesus' first twelve disciples by answering the riddles on the game sheet. Read each riddle and write the name of the correct person in the blank. Each disciple's name is used once. Use a Bible and a Bible storybook for hints.

---

1. Wezeman, Phyllis Vos and Judith Harris Chase. *Disciples Then! Disciples Now!* Prescott, Ariz.: Educational Ministries, Inc., 1995. Information adapted with permission.

Read each riddle and write the name of the correct person in the blank. Names to use include:

Andrew
Bartholomew/Nathanael
James the Greater
James the Less
John
Judas Iscariot
Jude/Thaddaeus
Matthew
Matthias
Philip
Simon Peter
Simon the Zealot
Thomas

1. Beloved disciple is what Jesus called me; I was one of the inner circle of three.
   Who am I? _____

2. My brother and I left our fishing behind; I brought others to Jesus, the Savior to find.
   Who am I? _____

3. My Lord and my God were the words that I said, when I believed that Jesus arose from the dead.
   Who am I? _____

4. Some people think bad thoughts when they hear my name. I betrayed the Savior and that is my shame.
   Who am I? _____

5. I always had questions and yet I still knew, Jesus was the Messiah; that's very true.
   Who am I? _____

6. Even a tax collector was chosen to serve. I wrote down the stories, God's love to preserve.
   Who am I? _____

7. People connect lots of numbers with me—one number is one and another is three.
   Who am I? _____

8. Although I was chosen at the very end, I always served Jesus and loved him as friend.
   Who am I? _____

9. One of my symbol's is the scallop shell. In the country of Spain they remember me well.
   Who am I? _____

10. Thaddaeus and Lebbaeus are two of my names, but a heart of compassion is my claim to fame.
    Who am I? _____

11. Strong willed is what they called the fighter in me; I wanted a kingdom that others could see.
    Who am I? _____

12. One name starts with N, and the other with a B; together they are part of my family history.
    Who am I? _____

13. Alphaeus is a word that's connected with me. Because others had my same first name, you see.
    Who am I? _____

Answers

1. John
2. Andrew
3. Thomas
4. Judas Iscariot
5. Philip
6. Matthew
7. Simon Peter
8. Matthias
9. James the Greater
10. Jude/Thaddaeus
11. Simon the Zealot
12. Bartholomew/Nathanael
13. James the Less

E

EXCAVATION

Purpose

To learn that archaeology is a method of uncovering events of the past and to participate in an archaeological "dig."

Preparation

Archaeological Definitions Game
- Archaeological Definitions Game sheets
- Duplicating equipment
- Paper
- Scissors

Classroom environment
- Tent
- Tables
- Patio blocks (optional)
- Archaeological tools and artifacts

"Dig" Equipment
- Pails
- Brushes, two different sizes
- Trowels
- Rulers
- Cardboard box lids
- Screen
- Duct tape
- Scissors
- Pencils
- Artifacts maps
- Clipboards (optional)

"Tell"
- Sand
- Sandbox, wading pool, or heavy plastic
- String
- Wooden stakes
- Index cards
- Markers
- Items to find

Advance Preparation

Archaeological Definitions Game
- Duplicate game sheet on page 28 and cut apart the cards. Be sure there is a card for each student.

Artifacts Map
- Duplicate map for each team of students.

Classroom Environment
- Create the setting of an archaeological dig in the classroom. Use any or all of these ideas to construct a simple or an elaborate environment. Set up a tent within the room as the headquarters of the dig. Place tables inside and around the tent to display tools, equipment, and artifacts associated with archaeologists: shovels, pails, flashlights, lanterns, brushes, and mess kits. If desired, the floor area could be laid with patio blocks to create a stone tile effect.

"Dig" Equipment
- Cut the screen into pieces slightly larger than the cardboard box lids and cover the edges with duct tape.
- Assemble equipment for each pair of students by placing two different sized brushes, a trowel, and a ruler in a pail. Place the pail and a piece of screen into a lid.

Tell
- Develop one area of the room as the "tell," a mound or hill-like formation of sand. Create the tell of play sand on heavy plastic or within a container such as a large sandbox or wading pool. Within the tell, hide artifacts for explorers to "discover" later. Some possible items to hide would be jewelry, pieces of broken clay pottery, cleaned bones, marbles, and old silver-ware. Make a grid to 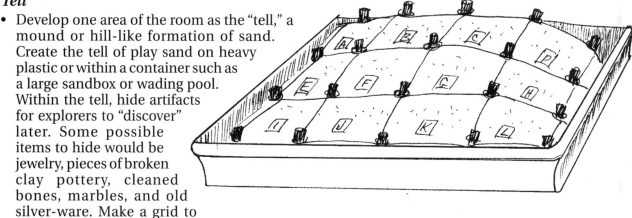 organize the excavation including the tell and surrounding area. Rope-off sections across the sand using string and wooden stakes. Label each section of the grid with a letter. Refer to the illustration for further ideas.

Procedure

Archaeology is the study of the human past through its material remains. Much has been learned about Bible times through archaeological expeditions to the Holy Land. In the city of Capernaum where Jesus made His home during part of His earthly ministry, archaeological excavations—called "digs"—have uncovered the remains of the synagogue where Jesus spoke and the home of Peter's mother-in-law, where one of Jesus' miracles took place. Provide the opportunity for the students to participate in an archaeological "dig" as a way to learn more about this process of "uncovering" the past.

Begin with a game to teach vocabulary. Distribute the Archaeological Definitions game cards and tell the students that half of the cards list key words related to archaeology and the other half contain definitions of these words. The goal of the game is for each player to find the person whose game piece matches theirs. Explain that they must find their archaeological partners without talking, that is, by using sign language or gestures to communicate. Once the matching puzzle piece is found, they are to read the definition and be ready to explain the term to the rest of the group. Be sure that adults observe and assist participants who are non-readers or who seem to need additional help.

When the matches have been made and the learners have had the opportunity to hear the definitions and seem to understand the terms, then invite them to participate in an archaeological dig. Lead the pupils to the tell, and ask them to sit on the floor with their partners and listen for further instructions.

Welcome the class to the tell. Ask a volunteer to tell what a tell is. Students should remember from the definitions that a tell is a hill-like formation resulting from the accumulation of layers of settlement or materials over a period of centuries. A tell is a place where archaeologists dig to find hints about how people once lived.

In order to experience how scientists have learned what life was like in Bible times—during the days of Peter and Jesus—invite the group to participate in a "dig." State that each team will receive a bucket containing brushes, a ruler, and a trowel, as well as a screen and a box. Explain the steps of the process. To begin the dig, brush sand from the tell into the trowel. Then use the trowel to empty the sand through the screen into the bucket. If any objects or artifacts are sifted out by the screen, use the smaller brush to clean the remaining sand from the artifact. Record the location, material, supposed purpose, and the size of the find on the team's artifacts map. Demonstrate each step of the process before proceeding. Verify understanding of the process before allowing the teams to begin the dig.

Distribute equipment and artifacts maps to the teams. Supervise the activity, expressing interest and delight over discoveries. When time is up, have students put away their tools and place their finds on a table or allow the pairs to divide up their treasures and take them home.

——— ARCHAEOLOGICAL DEFINITIONS GAME ———

Archaeology	**Archaeologist**	**Artifact**	**Excavation (Dig)**
Grid	**Sherds (Shards)**	**Strata**	**Tell (Tel)**
The study of the human past through its material remains.	A scientist who studies human life of the past, as revealed by artifacts left by ancient people.	Anything made, changed, or used in some way by a person or group of people.	A place where archaeologists work to find artifacts by digging and revealing them to view.
A pattern that organizes the excavation.	Broken pieces of pottery.	Horizontal layers of earth that represent different time periods.	A mound made by layers of settlement or materials over a period of centuries that contains the remains of ancient cities.

ARTIFACTS MAP

Dig Team Names: _____ _____

A	B	C	D
E	F	G	H
I	J	K	L

Remember to
1. Draw artifact on map
2. Write down name of material
3. Write down name and supposed purpose of artifact
4. Measure artifact in centimeters

A. _____

B. _____

C. _____

D. _____

E. _____

F. _____

G. _____

H. _____

I. _____

J. _____

K. _____

L. _____

F

FOOT WASHING

Purpose

To study the story of Jesus washing Peter's feet and to use a clown skit to experience the theme of servanthood.

Preparation

- Three chairs
- Rope
- Poster board
- Marker(s)
- Bucket
- Brushes of various sizes including a tooth brush
- Rags
- Plastic lids (4)
- Aluminum foil
- Hats: man's, woman's, child's cap, and beat-up hat
- "The Shoeshine" Script[1]

Advance Preparation

- Make four coins by wrapping foil around the plastic lids. On two coins write "five cents," and on the other two write "ten cents."

Procedure

This clown skit, based on John 13:1–17, in which Jesus washes the disciples' feet, is an especially effective way to convey the theme of servanthood—an important concept of clowning—and to learn more about the life of Peter.

Introduce the activity by reading the Scripture passage. Explain that during the Passover meal in the Upper Room, Jesus got up, put a towel on like an apron, poured water into a large bowl, and began to wash the disciples' feet. When Jesus came to Peter, Peter protested. Peter did not think that Jesus should be performing this lowly act. Instead, Peter thought that he should be washing the feet of Jesus. Jesus tells Peter that if He does not wash his feet, Peter is not in fellowship with Him. Peter responds by asking Jesus to wash him from head to toe! Explain that being a true disciple of Jesus—then and now—means serving one another as Jesus served us. To help understand this concept, use a clown skit to act out the theme.

If two people play all the roles, Clown One should play the shoe shiner and Clown Two should portray the remaining characters. Otherwise, five different people may present the skit. Involve everyone who is in the audience at the end. "The Shoe Shine" is most effective when done non-verbally.

---

1. Adapted with permission from a clown skit performed by "Lovely Lone Clowns," East United Methodist Church, Mishawaka, Indiana.

CLOWN 1

Enters a bare stage, which contains the three chairs. He is carrying a bucket filled with brushes, rags, markers; poster board; rope. He sets up a shoe shine stand by placing one chair center stage and the remaining two chairs behind it on either side of the stage. The rope is tied around the chair backs. He makes a sign that reads "Shoe Shine—10 Cents" and hangs it on the rope. When finished, he rests on the chair and waits for the first customer.

CLOWN 2

Enters wearing man's hat and carrying imaginary briefcase. Gestures that he would like his shoes shined, pays ten cents, and sits on chair.

CLOWN 1

Shines the shoes.

CLOWN 2

Exits.

CLOWN 3

Enters wearing woman's hat. Gestures that shoes should be shined, pays ten cents, and sits on chair.

CLOWN 1

Shines the shoes in a delicate way, such as by using the toothbrush.

CLOWN 3

Exits.

CLOWN 4

Enters wearing child's cap. Gestures for shoes to be shined. Pays five cents.

CLOWN 1

Points to shoe shine sign and gestures for more money.

CLOWN 4

Reluctantly pays other nickel. Sits on the chair.

CLOWN 1

Shines the shoes.

CLOWN 4

Exits.

CLOWN 5

Enters wearing beat-up hat. Gestures that he has no money and begs and pleads to have shoes shined.

CLOWN 1

Reluctantly gives in and gestures for clown five to sit down.

CLOWN 5

Sits down.

CLOWN 1

Shines shoes, but since they are so dirty, uses exaggerated movements and actions. After trying various brushes, he removes shoes from tramp's feet, scrubs them in the bucket, and hangs them on line or sets them on chair to dry.

CLOWN 5

Waits impatiently for shoes to dry. Pretends feet are very cold.

CLOWN 1

Since the shoes have not dried, the clown takes off his own shoes (sandals would be good), and places them on the feet of Clown Five.

CLOWN 5

Excitedly hugs Clown One and leaves.

CLOWN 1

Realizes how happy giving of himself for someone else has made him and changes sign to read "Shoe Shine—Free" rather than "10 Cents." At this point he begins to take people from the audience and cleans their shoes. He can also supply them with brushes and rags and send them through the group to "wash" other people's feet.

After the skit, apply the concept of servanthood to the theme of everyday life. Ask the participants to cite ways in which they can "wash feet" —that is, be servants. Examples could include raking leaves for an elderly neighbor, playing with a small child to give the parent a rest, or baking bread and delivering it as a gift.

G

GAMES

Purpose

To learn about the ups and downs of Peter's life by playing a game of "Fish Nets and Rope Ladders."

Preparation
- Game board
- Duplicating equipment
- Paper
- Poster board
- Spinner or die
- Playing pieces
- Scissors
- Glue

Advance Preparation
- Copy the game board onto plain paper and attach it to poster board.
- Borrow a spinner, numbered 1–6, from another game or use a die.

Procedure

Being a modern day disciple has many "ups" and "downs." Maybe that is why so many Christians identify with Peter—because of his many struggles in his efforts to follow Jesus. Peter's story is filled with glorious triumphs and disastrous blunders. Use the "Fish Nets and Rope Ladders" game to learn about some of the "ups" and "downs" of Peter's life as a disciple. Follow the directions and see who can change first from "follower" to "leader."

——— FISH NETS AND ROPE LADDERS RULES ———

Object of the Game

The object of the game is to be the first player to go from square number 1 to square number 50.

To Begin the Game

1. Each player chooses a different colored playing piece.
2. Each player spins the dial or throws the die to see who starts the game. The player with the highest number plays first. Other players follow in turn from left to right.

To Play

1. All players start their playing pieces just off the playing board next to square number 1 and move one square for each number spun on the dial. For example, if the spinner points to five, the playing piece is moved five squares. Each player has one turn at a time.
2. "Rope Ladders"—Should a player stop on a square at the bottom of a ladder, the player moves up to the square at the top of that ladder. Ladders only lead up.

3. "Fish Nets"—Should a playing piece land on a square at the top of a fish net, the player must move down to the square at the bottom of that chute. On the next turn, the player moves along from that position. Fish Nets only lead down.

4. The squares without ladders or nets are counted as regular squares.

5. Two or more players may stop on any square at the same time if their moves happen to land them in that position.

Winning the Game

1. Square 50 must be reached by an exact spin on the dial.
2. The first player to reach square 50 wins the game.

FISH NETS AND ROPE LADDERS GAME BOARD

Square 3.   Called by Jesus
Square 9.   Tries to walk on water
Square 11. Calls Jesus "Christ"
Square 19. "Get behind me Satan"
Square 23. Climbs mountain with Jesus
Square 26. Promises to feed Christ's sheep
Square 35. Talks rather than listens
Square 38. Shares Last Supper with Jesus
Square 44. Falls asleep in Garden
Square 45. Denial
Square 49. Hides in Upper Room
Square 50. Receives Holy Spirit at Pentecost

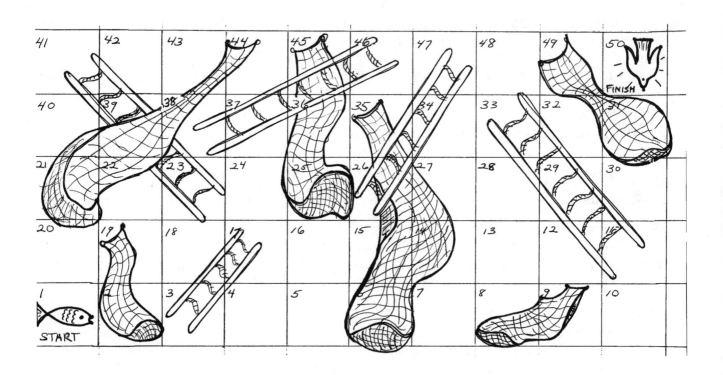

H

HOLY SPIRIT

Purpose

To experience Pentecost's life-changing power through poetry.

Preparation

- Paper
- Pencils or pens
- Bibles

Procedure

Prior to Pentecost, Peter often found himself failing to live up to the call of discipleship. Everyone knows of his famous boast to die at Jesus' side, and we know equally well of his three-fold denial when accused of being "one of them," a follower of the Galilean. In the beginning of the book of Acts, we find Peter hiding in the Upper Room behind locked doors. He and the other disciples lacked the direction and power to go on without their leader. But then comes the Spirit in mighty wind and tongues of flame. No more does he deny, or run away, or hide. Instead, a new Peter boldly braves the marketplace proclaiming a message of hope and salvation through Jesus Christ. What else can account for the change except a baptism of fire that burns away the old indecision and false facade of faith, and results in a new creature tempered to withstand the tests of true discipleship.

To understand the essence of the Pentecost story is to recognize the Holy Spirit's power to transform and enliven those who trust in Jesus the Savior. Poetry can provide a means of appreciating the power of Pentecost in the life of Peter and help us be more open to that Power in our own lives. A pattern for poetry called a "change poem" offers a method to help everyone explore thoughts and feelings in relation to Peter's and their own Pentecost story.

A "change poem" is a poem that begins with a noun that represents the person, place, thing, or idea as it exists originally, and ends with a synonym for that noun that demonstrates that a transformation has occurred. Any words between the first and last help the poet and the audience to visualize the change. Distribute paper and pencils or pens. Provide Bibles to share. Begin by having would-be poets play with pairs of words that represent a metamorphosis. For example, "Simon" could be paired with "Peter" and "disciple" with "apostle." Let them discuss what they see to be the difference that must occur between the two words in order to effect the change. These ideas then become the middle section of the poem. Any number of words or ideas may be used between the first and last words.

An example of a "change" poem related to the life of Peter is

Disciple . . .
A student
follows the Teacher
listening,
learning,
growing.
Troubled,

forgiven.
Waiting for
a new Power —
a wind to test new wings —
Bursts from the upper schoolroom
into the marketplace, an
Apostle.

Allow time for individuals or small groups to write "change" poems related to Peter's Pentecost experience. Invite volunteers to read their words or post the creative writing on a bulletin board for all to see.

I

IDENTIFICATION

Purpose
To define words and explain symbols used to identify early Christians and to design a personal ID tag.

Preparation
- Leather identification tag kits or cowhide "blanks" available at hobby and craft shops
- Beaded key chains or split rings
- Scrap paper
- Pencils
- Leather supplies for stamping or tooling (substitute for leather tools: cuticle sticks made of orange wood)
- Scissors
- Mallet or block of wood
- Drive punch or leather rotary punch
- Clean sponges
- Water
- Neutral shoe polish or paste wax
- Clean rags
- Rulers

Procedure
During the time of the early Christian church it was dangerous to be a follower of Jesus. Christians met secretly to worship. In order to avoid being arrested by Roman soldiers, early disciples used a simple fish image as a secret code to mark a meeting place or as a way to identify each other. The five Greek letters that form the word "fish" are the first letters of the five words: "Jesus Christ God's Son Savior" in Greek.

Greek letters: ΙΧΘΥΣ
Our alphabet: ICHTHUS

Christians throughout history have used the initials and the fish symbol as a sign of faith. One of the symbols attributed to Peter is a fish (Mark 1:16–18). Design a leather identification tag with a fish symbol to proclaim your faith to others, as well as to mark personal items.

Tooling or stamping processes have been used for hundreds of years to decorate leather. Stamps are metal posts used to imprint patterns and letters into the leather's surface. The end of the stamp may have an engraved or raised design. Some suppliers may have leather stamps with the Christian fish symbol. To stamp a design, dampen the leather on both sides with a sponge and place it smooth side up on a hard surface. Allow the top to dry a little, since leather that is too wet will not retain the impressed shapes. Hold the metal stamp upright and tap firmly with a hammer or mallet. Form the shape of a fish and stamp your name or initials on the piece, too.

Tooling is a way of modeling leather with a metal or wooden tool that is pointed on one end and flat on the other. The pointed end, curved upward, is used for outlining and stippling. The flat end is used to make depressed areas on the leather's surface.

Dampen the leather on both sides and work on a hard surface with the right side up. Use the narrow end of the modeling tool and press firmly to outline a fish shape. Carefully print name or initials for personal identification. To depress the fish shape, rub the flat end of the tool back and forth within the outlined area. Dampen the leather again, if necessary. Continue until the design and letters are permanently impressed into the leather.

When the stamping or tooling is finished, allow the leather to dry thoroughly. Punch necessary holes to turn the finished piece into a key chain or ring. Protect the leather with neutral shoe polish or paste wax. Buff with a soft rag. If using a kit, follow directions for finishing.

Attach the identification tag to a gym bag, notebook, or other personal item. Know that the simple fish symbol links you with Christians today as well as with Peter and with all of the early followers of Jesus.

J

JOURNEY

Purpose
To trace the steps of Peter's journey of faith.

Preparation
- "Peter's Journey" sheet
- Paper
- Duplicating equipment
- Pencils or pens
- Bibles
- Construction paper, 12" x 18" sheets & scraps
- Scissors
- Glue
- Markers
- Footprint pattern

Advance Preparation
- Duplicate "Peter's Journey" sheet.

Procedure
It is said that the best way to get to know another person is to walk in that individual's shoes. Although we cannot literally place our feet into the shoes—probably sandals—of Peter, we can retrace his steps and learn about his life.

Turning to Scripture, history, and tradition to recreate Peter's journey of faith, we learn that—among other things—Peter was a believer, disciple, family member, fisherman, leader, martyr, missionary, preacher, witness, and writer. Use this information as the basis of an activity to depict Peter's journey.

Trace Peter's steps by reading the statements on the activity sheet, looking up the Scripture references, and choosing one word from the list that describes that specific part of Peter's journey. Write the word in the blank that best completes the sentence.

Read each statement, look up the Scripture references, and choose one word from the list that best completes the sentence. Each word is used once.

Word List
Believer
Disciple
Eyewitness
Family member
Fisherman
Leader
Martyr
Missionary
Preacher
Writer

Statements

1. As the son of John (John 21:15), the brother of Andrew (Mark 1:16), a son-in-law (Mark 1:30), and a husband (1 Corinthians 9:5), Peter was a _____.
2. As a partner in a business in Bethsaida and Capernaum, Peter was a _____ (Matthew 4:18–20).
3. Peter, probably an early follower of John the Baptist (Acts 1:22), was called to be a _____ of Jesus (Matthew 4:18–22).
4. Peter the _____ proclaimed Jesus to be the Christ, the Son of God (Matthew 16:16).
5. Peter was an _____ to the miracles of Jesus (Mark 1:30) and to the resurrection (Luke 24:12).
6. Peter was the _____ of the disciples (Mark 3:13–19), the group gathered at Jerusalem (Acts 1:15), and the early Christian church (Acts 2:43–4:37).
7. Peter the _____ proclaimed the Gospel on Pentecost (Acts 2:14–41).
8. Peter was a _____ who traveled to places such as Lydda (Acts 9:32–35), Joppa (Acts 9:36–42), Caesarea (Acts 11:1–18), Antioch (Galatians 2:11), and Rome (1 Peter 5:13).
9. Peter was a _____ who authored two epistles in the New Testament (1 Peter and 2 Peter) and who probably provided information to Mark for his gospel.
10. Tradition claims that Peter was a _____ for Christ when he was crucified in Rome.

Answers

1. Family member
2. Fisherman
3. Disciple
4. Believer
5. Eyewitness
6. Leader
7. Preacher
8. Missionary
9. Writer
10. Martyr

When the activity sheet is completed, use the answers to trace Peter's journey of faith in the form of a mini-banner. Using the pattern provided, trace the footprint onto construction paper and cut out at least ten footsteps. Print one answer from the "Peter's Journey" activity sheet on each shape. Include Scripture references, key ideas, or simple drawings, if desired. Attach the footprints to a 12" x 18" sheet of construction paper in an order that illustrates Peter's journey of faith.

Caption the mini-banner "Follow Me." Look up Mark 1:17 and John 21:22. Isn't it interesting that Jesus' first and last words to Simon Peter were "Follow me." Look at the words on the footprints and take time to think about or write ways in which they apply to each participant's personal journey of faith.

K

KINGDOM

Purpose
To remember our responsibility of staying open to God's leadership, symbolized by the keys we carry.

Preparation
- Patterns for keys, various sizes
- Construction paper
- Scissors
- Ribbon, narrow (four colors, if desired)
- Pencils
- Markers
- Bible
- Hole punch

Procedure
While few countries are truly governed by monarchs anymore, most of us understand the concept of a supreme ruler like a king. In Jesus' day, of course, the idea of the kingdom of God communicated even more easily. The king was the one who held absolute power over your life, the one who issued the money, raised the armies, declared war and peace, and deserved your allegiance and loyalty. His kingdom was the territory encompassed by that authority. However, earthly kings have limits on their power. To think of God as a monarch is to imagine a dominion without limits. But God's eternal dominion is spiritual, invisible; as Jesus said, it can only be entered by faith.

The idea of God as our King or Sovereign must also be considered in light of Jesus' explanation that God is our Father. In other words, we are children of the King, and we have certain responsibilities in the territory that our parental monarch governs. In Matthew 16, Peter earns the keys to the kingdom when he recognizes who Jesus really is, a sign to Jesus that Peter is listening to the voice of his heavenly Father. Upon Peter's proclamation of faith, Jesus revealed His plan for a church on which Satan's gates could never close. Peter used the keys at Pentecost and opened the door for thousands to receive Christ. Later Peter used the keys with Cornelius, the centurion, and opened the door for Gentiles to follow Christ.

This story from Peter's life offers us some "keys" to understanding what we, as present-day children of the King, are expected to do.

- Key One — Listen to God
- Key Two — Know Jesus as Christ
- Key Three — Worship with others who listen to God
- Key Four — Unlock any doors that keep people from God

Read the story in Matthew 16. Discuss how Peter came to know who Jesus really was. Explain the importance of Peter's willingness to risk saying aloud what he believed about Jesus. Point out that the church is built upon the faith of those who gather to speak aloud their belief in God as revealed in Jesus Christ. Explore what keys symbolize. To whom do we give keys and why? In what ways do people get "locked out" from God? How can the church let people know that the doorway to God is always open?

For an activity, make a set of keys as a reminder of who we are, and use the keys as symbols to discuss the power and responsibility of God's children. Adapt the complexity of the craft and discussion depending on age or ability levels. For elementary children, it is enough to use the patterns provided and cut key shapes from construction paper. Write on each shape one "key" idea such as "Listen to God," "Know Jesus Christ," "Worship with Others," and "Open Locked Doors." Punch a hole at the top of each key, thread the shapes onto heavy cord, knot the ends, and use the piece as a necklace. For older youth, make a ribbon Bible bookmark, attaching smaller construction-paper "keys" to each of four different ribbons. Write the "key" idea on each, as explained above. Tie the four strands together at the top. For adults, use the discussion questions to share and explore what it means to be entrusted with the keys to the kingdom.

"Key" Discussion Questions:

1. How do you enter the "kingdom within" to listen for God's voice?
2. What does it mean to you to say that Jesus is the Christ, the Son of the Living God?
3. Whom do you know that listens to God with you?
4. What kinds of doors or barriers keep people from God? And how can you keep the pathways open?

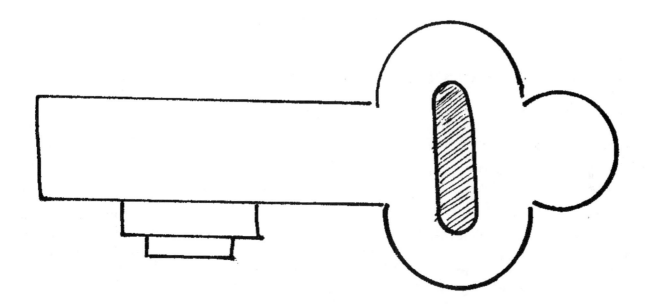

L

LIFE

Purpose

To suggest age-appropriate activities that will provide visual information related to the important events in Peter's life.

Preparation

- List of Scripture passages describing significant happenings in Peter's life
- Bibles, concordances, and commentaries for children and adults
- Materials vary according to project

Procedure

Three learning experiences are suggested—one each for children, youth, and adults—to teach information about the life of Peter in age-appropriate ways.

CHILDREN: "WONDER BOX"

Preparation

- Box
- Objects, pictures, and symbols that relate to various parts of Peter's story

Advance Preparation

- Prepare the "Wonder Box." Decorate the outside of the box, if desired. Place objects, pictures, and symbols related to Peter's story inside the box.

Introduce young participants to the stories of Peter's life. Tell of his importance as a friend to Jesus and as a leader of the first Christians. Use a children's Bible or storybook to help relate the material in terms young learners will understand.

Explain that as the story is told, participants will see a surprise from the "Wonder Box." The object or picture will help them remember information about Peter. Pull out items as the story unfolds: fish, keys, rooster, rock, sheep, cross. Include pictures of Jesus, Sea of Galilee, types of sailing ships used for fishing or for traveling to Rome, Saint Peter's Basilica and other monuments. What other objects will help tell about Peter's life?

YOUTH: BULLETIN BOARD OR GRAFFITI WALL

Preparation

- Bibles and reference materials
- Pencils
- Paper
- Wide-tip markers
- Paint
- Brushes

- Butcher paper
- Tape

Familiarize the group with the use of Bible study guides, such as concordances, commentaries, and Bible dictionaries. List different topics dealing with Peter's life and instruct groups or individuals to find related Scripture passages. Subject matter may include some of the following:

- Called to become a disciple
- Declares that Jesus is the Christ
- Denies Jesus
- Sees the risen Lord
- Gives sermon at Pentecost
- Continues Jesus' teachings

Encourage students to explore the different resources. Allow time to share information. Choose the most important or pivotal points in Peter's life and record the Scripture references on a bulletin board or "graffiti" wall.

Cover the bulletin board or wall with paper from a large roll such as butcher paper. The graffiti may be in sequence or scattered. The wall should include references from all aspects of Peter's life to provide a complete profile of who he was, his relationship to Jesus, and his importance to the early Christian church. Draw simple pictures to illustrate the verses.

—— ADULT: TIME-LINE ——

Preparation
- Bibles
- Concordances, commentaries, and other resources
- Markers
- Poster board or roll of paper

Adult classes following a course of study or series of lessons on the life of Peter might find it helpful to develop some visual aids. As the lessons progress, develop a time-line. Arrange, in sequence, brief phrases, simple illustrations, maps, and symbols to give a visual summary of Peter's life and ministry. Topics may include those mentioned in the Youth section plus others.

For an intergenerational study of Peter, consider dramatizing his life by presenting a "Man on the Street" interview by asking questions about Peter's ministry to a variety of people or stage a "This Is Your Life" program where participants pretend to be acquaintances of Peter and share information about his life. These events can be entertaining as well as educational!

M

MUSIC

Purpose
To use music as a teaching tool to address the topics and themes of Peter's life.

Preparation
- Music for selected songs
- Accompaniment (optional)
- Hymnals
- Paper
- Pens
- Bibles

Procedure
Tell the story of Peter's life or teach a theme related to his legacy through music. Write new words to an existing tune and sing the Scripture! Suggestions are offered for children and adults.

For children, compose new words to the song "Michael, Row The Boat Ashore." Sing the first verse of the song together to be sure everyone knows the tune. Then create new verses based on the Bible stories and themes related to Peter's life. Start with these sample verses and make up more! Be sure to repeat each phrase four times.

- Jesus said, "Come, Follow Me." Alleluia.
- Jesus calmed the angry sea. Alleluia.
- Jesus rose up from the grave. Alleluia.
- Jesus told me, "Feed My Sheep." Alleluia.

For youth and adults, sing a new hymn text based on Matthew 14:22–31, "When Life's Storms Are Too Insistent!"

When Life's Storms Are Too Insistent!
Text: John A. Dalles [Copyright © 1996, John A. Dalles]
Tune: TRUST IN JESUS*
Meter: 8.7.8.7 with refrain

When life's storms are too insistent,
Call us, Lord, to come to You!
When the shore seems grey and distant,
Call us, Lord, to come to You!

Refrain:
    May we come to You, Lord Jesus!
    Call us, Lord, to come to You!
    Catch and keep us in Your presence:
    Call us, Lord, to come to You!

When the waves all beat around us,
Call us, Lord, to come to You!
When the head-wind gusts confound us,
Call us, Lord, to come to You!

(Refrain)

When we cry in fearful sorrow.
Call us, Lord, to come to You!
When we drift from You afar, O!
Call us, Lord, to come to You!

(Refrain)

When we sense that we are sinking,
Call us, Lord, to come to You!
Then, Your arms around us linking,
Call us, Lord, to come to You!

(Refrain)

The words of this hymn may be reprinted without special permission provided that the following acknowledgment is included: From *Ideas A–Z: Peter*. Words © 1996 John A. Dalles. Used by permission.

As an additional or alternate activity, use music to highlight the key events of Peter's life. Compile a list of six to ten Scripture passages that tell Peter's story in chronological order. Refer to the "Where" section of *Ideas A–Z: Peter* for references. Then using a hymnal, find a song that communicates each theme. For example:

- Peter is called by Jesus—Matthew 4:18–22
- "Jesus Calls Us"

- Peter witnesses Jesus' miracles and ministry—Matthew 8:14–17
- "Thine Arm, O Lord, in Days of Old"

- Peter confesses Jesus as the Messiah—Matthew 16:13–20
- "Beautiful Savior"

- Peter denies Jesus—Matthew 26:69–75
- "In the Hour of Trial"

- Peter is an eyewitness to the resurrection—John 20:2–10
- "Christ Arose"

---

* "'Tis So Sweet to Trust in Jesus"

- Peter is commissioned by Jesus—John 21:1–22
- "My Jesus, I Love Thee"

- Peter is filled with the Holy Spirit on Pentecost—Acts 2:13–42
- "O for a Thousand Tongues to Sing"

- Peter tells others about Jesus—Acts 10:1–48
- "I Love to Tell the Story"

Once the list is compiled, make arrangements for various people to read the Scripture passages and for an instrumentalist to accompany the singing. Explain to the group that the story of Peter's life will be shared through Scripture and song. Someone will read Bible verses related to part of Peter's life. Invite the group to listen to the words and to respond by singing a song associated with the theme. For variety, soloists may also share the musical messages. Enjoy a time of telling Peter's story in this unique way.

N

NUMBERS

Purpose
To use numbers as answers to a crossword puzzle about Peter's life.

Preparation
- Crossword puzzle
- Pencils
- Bibles
- Duplicating equipment
- Paper

Advance Preparation
- Duplicate crossword puzzles.

Procedure
One. Two. Three. Fifty. Three thousand. Many numbers come to mind when one thinks about the life of Simon Peter. As number one, he and his brother Andrew were the first disciples to be called to follow Jesus. During the course of his ministry, Jesus gave Simon a second name, Peter, for a special reason. Peter's words, recorded in Matthew 16:16; Mark 8:29; and Luke 9:20, form the basis for the creeds and confessions of the church today. Three times Peter denied Jesus and three times Peter was assured of Jesus' love and forgiveness. Fifty days after Jesus' resurrection, on the day of Pentecost, Peter was filled with the Holy Spirit and preached a powerful sermon, resulting in the conversion of at least three thousand new believers.

These numbers, and others, form the structure for clues in a crossword puzzle about Peter. Use the project to help participants learn more about the countless ways in which Peter's ministry and mission influenced the early church and the church today. Distribute a copy of the crossword puzzle and a pencil to each student. Offer Bibles for those who need additional help.

Across

2. Confession recorded in Matthew _____
5. One of the first _____ disciples
7. Denied Jesus _____ times
8. _____ names: Simon and Peter
9. _____ symbols: bishop's miter, fish, keys, rock, roster, shepherd's staff

Down

1. Preached _____ days after Easter
3. _____ were baptized on Pentecost
4. Story recorded in _____ Gospels
6. Proclaimed Jesus as the _____ Messiah

Answers Across: 2. Sixteen; 5. Twelve; 7. Three; 8. Two; 9. Six. **Down:** 1. Fifty; 3. Three Thousand; 4. Four; 6. One.

O

OVERHEAD PROJECTOR

Purpose
To explore ways that an overhead projector can be used to create a setting and develop an environment.

Preparation
- Bibles
- Encyclopedias, Bible atlases, maps, and other resources that provide drawings or photos of scenes along the seaside as well as illustrations of a fisherman's way of life
- Overhead projector
- Transparencies
- Markers
- Large pieces of background materials (fabric, wide rolls of butcher paper, large sheets of foam board or cardboard)
- Tempera paints
- Large paint brushes
- Giant-sized chalk
- Pencils
- Paper
- Tape
- Clean-up supplies

Procedure
Peter's story will come to life and leave a lasting impression on learners if a stimulating environment is part of the activities. Create an exciting setting that appeals to all of the senses! Peter's early life as a fisherman would have been filled with many sensory experiences.

Include murals of fishing boats, lake shore scenes, and fishing villages for visual interest; listen to tapes of water and seashore sounds; consider using real fish to provide the smells; plan a fish fry or introduce other tastes of the region; gather shells, nets, baskets, sand, and nautical gear for a rich variety of textures. Is there a body of water nearby? Can you find small wooden boats, pilings, or canvas sails? Add any available props to simulate a seaport environment.

After studying photos and illustrations from several resources, use an overhead projector to create transparencies to use as backdrops. Follow these simple steps:

1. Choose simple line drawings, trace photos, or create original drawings.
2. Transfer outlines to acetate transparency sheet by
   - using photocopier which is able to make transparencies;
   - using a Thermo-Fax machine;
   - tracing with special markers directly onto the transparency.
3. Place transparency with transferred scene onto the "stage" or glass platform of the overhead projector.
4. Position the projector and adjust the focus knob to get the desired image size and clarity. (Overhead projectors enable you to change image size. Move closer to reduce; pull back to enlarge.)

5. Test projected image on screen or blank wall.
6. Attach paper, fabric, cardboard or foam board to wall and trace projected outline with pencil, marker, or chalk.
7. Color the traced scene with paint or chalk. It may be easier to remove the scene from the wall and continue working on tables or the floor.
8. Use large brushes and tempera paint or sidewalk chalk to complete the scenery. Details are not necessary if the murals are viewed from a distance.

Follow the same procedure, on a smaller scale, to design bulletin boards. If space is limited, place murals on the back of a piano, on doors, room dividers, or easels. Experiment with tissue paper, colored cellophane, and paints to decorate windows. Be creative!

A great deal of learning occurs as students research what life was like for a fisherman in a seaport town. As each sense is awakened and as each setting is developed, learners will have a greater understanding of Peter and the life he led.

P

PRISON

Purpose
To use an action story to teach about Peter's imprisonment and release.

Preparation
- Action story script
- Chalkboard or newsprint
- Chalk or markers
- Bible

Procedure
Peter told many people about Jesus and the church grew and grew. Some of the rulers did not want people to believe in Jesus, so they told Peter to stop preaching and teaching. Several times Peter was put in prison because he continued to tell people about God's love. Stories of Peter's imprisonments are recorded in Acts 4:1–31; Acts 5:17–42; and Acts 12:1–19.

Tell the Acts 12:1–19 account of Peter's imprisonment using an action story that includes movements and gestures to illustrate each line. This method involves learners in the process and assures that the Bible story is memorable and meaningful.

To tell an action story, have the group of listeners sit or stand facing the leader who tells the story and demonstrates all motions for the participants. Words to be repeated can be written out on newsprint or on a chalkboard, or can simply be emphasized with the voice so that hearers understand the key words to recite. Additional movements and gestures may be improvised by the group or the leader.

PETER'S IMPRISONMENT

Peter kept proclaiming the message of Jesus

[Cup hands to mouth]

Until one day the rulers had him arrested and put in prison.

[Cross wrists to symbolize chains]

But his friends in the church prayed for him.

[Fold hands in prayer gesture]

One night as he slept

[Place both hands on side of face and close eyes]

With prison guards watching him

[Cup one hand over eyes]

Suddenly an angel appeared.

[Extend arms in gesture of surprise]

Peter's chains fell away.

[Uncross wrists and move arms down]

Peter and the angel walked right past the guards.

[Walk in place]

In the cool night air

[Wrap arms around self]

Peter realized he wasn't dreaming.

[Place hands on cheeks]

Peter walked to the house where his friends met for church.

[Walk in place]

He knocked and knocked on the door.

[Knock]

When Rhoda, the servant girl, opened the door

[Gesture opening door]

She was so surprised she slammed the door and ran away.

[Slam door and run in place]

Peter knocked again.

[Knock]

This time all his friends came to see who was at the door.

[Open door]

Imagine their joy when they realized

[Cross hands over heart]

Peter was truly free.

[Extend arms wide]

Q

QUESTIONS

Purpose

To use a computer software program to identify questions that Jesus asked Peter and the other disciples and to provide a personal answer to these biblical questions.

Preparation

- Computer with Bible software
- Highlighting markers
- Blank paper and color markers or poster paint

Procedure

Like any good teacher, Jesus used probing questions to help to the disciples think deeply about important spiritual issues. Use a computer software program that allows you to search the text of the Bible for words or phrases (the King James Version text is commonly available; other modern translation are also available). If a computer can be used in the classroom, have a participant or group conduct the search (practice with the program beforehand so you are familiar with it!). Look for words such as *what* or *who* in the Gospels. If a computer is not available in the teaching setting, do the search beforehand and print out a list of the verses that can be copied and distributed to the group.

You may want to limit your search to one of the Gospels. For example, Matthew has 220 uses of "what" in the King James Version text. When you have assembled a list of "what" or "who" verses and printed them, divide the participants into small groups. Have each group go through the list with highlighting markers and identify verses with questions Jesus asked using the search word. See which group can correctly identify all the questions. Discuss together the various questions.

- What question was the most personal?
- What question would have made listeners angry at Jesus?
- What question would you most want to know the answer to?

After identifying all the questions and discussing them, have each person pick one question and make a small poster to take with them. Have them write out the question on a sheet of blank paper and fill in the sheet with designs and color. When the posters are done, have volunteers share their thoughts on why a particular question was important to them and how they would respond to Jesus.

Question Search in Matthew

Matt. 2:7   Then Herod, when he had privily called the wise men, inquired of them diligently what time the star appeared.

Matt. 5:46   For if ye love them which love you, **what** reward have ye? do not even the publicans the same?

Matt. 5:47   And if ye salute your brethren only, **what** do ye more than others? do not even the publicans so?

Matt. 6:3	But when thou doest alms, let not thy left hand know what thy right hand doeth:
Matt. 6:8	Be not ye therefore like unto them: for your Father knoweth what things ye have need of, before ye ask him.
Matt. 6:25	Therefore I say unto you, Take no thought for your life, **what** ye shall eat, or **what** ye shall drink; nor yet for your body, **what** ye shall put on. Is not the life more than meat, and the body than raiment?
Matt. 6:31	Therefore take no thought, saying, What shall we eat? or, What shall we drink? or, Wherewithal shall we be clothed?
Matt. 7:2	For with **what** judgment ye judge, ye shall be judged: and with what measure ye mete, it shall be measured to you again.
Matt. 7:9	Or what man is there of you, whom if his son ask bread, will he give him a stone?
Matt. 8:27	But the men marvelled, saying, What manner of man is this, that even the winds and the sea obey him!
Matt. 8:29	And, behold, they cried out, saying, What have we to do with thee, Jesus, thou Son of God? art thou come hither to torment us before the time?
Matt. 8:33	And they that kept them fled, and went their ways into the city, and told every thing, and what was befallen to the possessed of the devils.
Matt. 9:13	But go ye and learn what that meaneth, I will have mercy, and not sacrifice: for I am not come to call the righteous, but sinners to repentance.
Matt. 10:19	But when they deliver you up, take no thought how or what ye shall speak: for it shall be given you in that same hour what ye shall speak.
Matt. 10:27	What I tell you in darkness, that speak ye in light: and what ye hear in the ear, that preach ye upon the housetops.
Matt. 11:7	And as they departed, Jesus began to say unto the multitudes concerning John, **What** went ye out into the wilderness to see? A reed shaken with the wind?
Matt. 11:8	But **what** went ye out for to see? A man clothed in soft raiment? behold, they that wear soft clothing are in kings' houses.
Matt. 11:9	But **what** went ye out for to see? A prophet? yea, I say unto you, and more than a prophet.
Matt. 12:3	But he said unto them, Have ye not read what David did, when he was an hungered, and they that were with him;
Matt. 12:7	But if ye had known what this meaneth, I will have mercy, and not sacrifice, ye would not have condemned the guiltless.
Matt. 12:11	And he said unto them, **What** man shall there be among you, that shall have one sheep, and if it fall into a pit on the sabbath day, will he not lay hold on it, and lift it out?
Matt. 16:26	For **what** is a man profited, if he shall gain the whole world, and lose his own soul? or **what** shall a man give in exchange for his soul?

R

ROCKS

Purpose
To describe the significance of rocks in important occasions of Peter's life.

Preparation
- Smooth pebbles, beach stones, or flat rocks
- Shallow, flat dish, tray, or basket
- Permanent markers with fine tips or calligraphy tips
- Bible
- Picture atlas and other reference materials
- Plants (optional)

Procedure
Several of the disciples were known by new names when they became followers of Jesus. Peter was named by his family Simon Bar-Jona or Simon, son of John. After Simon declared to the disciples that their leader was the Messiah (Matthew 16:16), Jesus referred to this special disciple by the Aramaic surname of *Kepha*, which means rock. Using Greek letters to transliterate the word, it comes out Cephas. Translated into Greek the word is *Petros*. The Greek counterpart becomes Peter in English. Matthew 16:18 records Jesus' conferring of the descriptive title: "And I tell you that you are Peter, and on this rock I will build my church, and the gates of Hades will not overcome it" (NIV). Jesus declared that Peter's confession would be the solid foundation, or the rock, of the future church. Peter was a constant companion of Jesus and some of the highlights of his life as an apostle involve rocks or stones.

Look up the following passages and learn about Peter:

- Matthew 14:28–33 . . . Peter attempts to walk on the water
- Matthew 16:13–19 . . . Peter's name, character, confession
- Matthew 17:1–8 . . . Peter witnesses the Transfiguration
- John 20:1–10 . . . Peter at the tomb after the Resurrection
- John 21:10–17 . . . Peter and Jesus—breakfast by the sea
- Luke 24:50–53 . . . Peter observes Jesus' ascension

After reading the passages, look through Bible atlases and other reference books to understand the geography of the area.

There are stones everywhere! Scenes of landscape, seashore, and buildings consist of rocks, pebbles, or boulders. Envision Peter at the seashore. There were probably rocks in the water when he began to sink after attempting to walk toward Jesus. When Jesus and the disciples cooked breakfast on the beach, the fire pit was most likely formed with rocks.

Peter was among the first witnesses to see the empty tomb after Jesus' resurrection. Following His crucifixion, Jesus was buried in a cave, which was sealed with a large boulder. Imagine the questions Peter had when he saw the heavy rock rolled away.

The Scriptures report that Peter was present at two more important events in the life of Jesus: the

Transfiguration and the Ascension. The Transfiguration took place on a mountain, which was a rocky site. In Luke, it is reported that Jesus led the followers to Bethany, then ascended into heaven. Pictures of surroundings will show stone buildings and rocky landscape.

Arrange a simple display of rocks as reminders of the high points of Peter's life as someone especially chosen by Jesus. Read carefully the Scripture passages and try to picture the scenes. Use a permanent marker to print or a calligraphy pen to letter the chapter and verse references. Print a few key words or draw a picture to indicate the main elements of the passage.

Place the stones in a shallow dish, basket, or tray. The stones may serve as story or prayer prompters or as a sequencing activity. Add a small plant or tiny bouquet of flowers for color and use the arrangement in a personal or classroom worship center.

S

SCRIPTURE

Purpose
To use photographic techniques to illustrate miracle stories involving Jesus and Peter.

Preparation
Supplies will vary with selected activities.

Procedure
During Peter's years as a disciple, a student of the Great Teacher, he witnessed Jesus perform many miracles. In the company of His first followers Jesus healed Peter's mother-in-law (Matthew 8:15; Mark 1:31; Luke 4:39), raised Jairus' daughter from the dead (Matthew 9:25; Mark 5:41; Luke 8:54), and restored sight to the man born blind (John 9:7). As an apostle, one commissioned by Christ to spread the Gospel, Peter performed miracles, too. Acts 3:6–8 records the story of healing a lame man, Acts 5:15 tells of healing many people, Acts 9:32–34 documents the healing of Aeneas, and Acts 9:36–41 chronicles the raising of Dorcas from the dead.

Teach the miracle stories involving Jesus and Peter, as well as any other Scripture lessons, by portraying the significant events of the passage through procedures involving photography or projection. Make or take the pictures using overhead, video, slide, and print techniques. Try a different method for a series of weeks or vary the mode throughout the year.

OVERHEAD PROJECTOR

Preparation
- Overhead projector
- Screen
- Acetate transparencies
- Permanent markers
- Bibles

Procedure
Look up the story of the miracle of the coin in the fish's mouth in Matthew 17:24–27. Review the incident related to Peter and the tax. When the officials came to collect the tax from Jesus, there was no money to give them. Jesus instructed Peter to go fishing and said that there would be a coin in the mouth of the first fish he caught. When Peter opened the fish's mouth he found a coin, and he paid the taxes that were due.

Illustrate the story by using permanent markers and drawing pictures on acetate transparencies. Scenes to include could be

- Tax collectors asking Peter for money;
- Peter telling them he has no money;
- Jesus telling Peter to go fishing;
- Peter catching a fish;

- Peter finding a coin in the fish's mouth;
- Peter paying the tax.

Show the pictures on the overhead projector and retell, recite, or read the passage that records this miracle.

PHOTOGRAPHS

Preparation
- Camera
- Film
- Bulletin board
- Pins, tacks, or tape

Procedure
Review the Gospels and the book of Acts for additional miracle stories involving Jesus and Peter. Read several of these accounts and discuss ways in which God's power was demonstrated through these events. Consider ways in which God's power is shown by modern day disciples: us. Examples could include serving a meal at a soup kitchen, visiting a patient in a nursing home, and volunteering at a homeless center.

Take pictures to illustrate these "modern-day miracles." Display the photographs on a bulletin board as reminders that Jesus' followers today are responsible for sharing God's love with others.

SLIDES

Preparation
- Acetate transparencies
- Slide mounts
- Scissors
- Markers
- Slide projector
- Screen
- Bible

Procedure
Make slides to teach a miracle story such as Peter walking on the water, recorded in Matthew 14:22–33. Cut pieces of acetate transparency to fit the slide mounts. Draw an illustration of a different part of the story on each piece, for example:

- Jesus goes to the mountain to pray;
- The disciples are in the boat during a storm at sea;
- Jesus walks on the water towards the disciples;
- The disciples are afraid;
- Jesus tells the disciples to be calm;
- Peter challenges Jesus to let him walk on the water, too;
- Jesus tells Peter to come to Him;
- Peter walks on the water towards Jesus;
- Peter becomes frightened and begins to sink;
- Peter cries to Jesus to save him;
- Jesus extends His hand to Peter and catches him.

When the illustrations are completed, place the acetate pieces in the slide mounts. Put the slides in order, project the images on the screen, and look at the story in a new way.

Preparation

- Video camera
- Video tape
- VCR and monitor
- Bible times costumes
- Bible

Procedure

Pick a miracle story that would be easy to act out, such as Peter, John, and the beggar. Read the Scripture passage in Acts 3:1–10. Once there was a lame man who sat at the gate to the temple and begged people to give him money. Peter and John told the man they could not give him money; they could give him something better. Peter said, "In the name of Jesus, walk." Peter took the man by the hand and helped him up. The man could walk again. The man and the people who witnessed this miracle praised God for His power.

Dress in Bible-times costumes, portray the people, and video tape their stories as individuals or as a group. Share the interviews as a way to teach this lesson.

T

TASTE

Purpose

To create a flavorful memory of the life of Peter.

Preparation

- Plates
- Napkins
- Glasses
- Water
- Cooking and serving equipment (varied per snack)
- Ingredients (varied per snack)

Procedure

Many stories of the disciples and Jesus had to do with sharing meals. Whether the event was as elaborate as a wedding feast or as simple as the shelling of grain with their palms, Jesus used the experience of sharing food as an opportunity to teach His disciples about God. Good teachers today recognize the value of using the sense of taste as a method of making memories to ensure learning. Peter's life story is so connected to the sea that fish seem the obvious choice to create a meaningful memory for modern-day students. In fact, there is even a fish named for him, the "Saint Peter fish."

Tradition has it that after Peter caught the fish with the coin in its mouth for the tax (Matthew 17:24–27) this particular type of fish continued to bear the mark of a coin on its side, hence its name the "Saint Peter fish." As well, many countries have a tradition of eating fish on Saint Peter's feast day, June 29, and of giving fish to the poor in his name.

To celebrate a study of Peter, create a feast with fish as the main course or use fish—in many forms—as a snack during a lesson. Make the menu simple or elaborate, but be sure to create the connection to the life of Peter. Add bread, dates, grapes, raisins, nuts, olives, or cheese to complete the snack or meal as desired. Serve water as the drink.

For simple celebrations:
- Fish-shaped crackers
- Canned or smoked fish
- Tuna fish sandwiches
- Tuna casserole
- Fish soup
- Fish shaped gummy candy

For more elaborate celebrations:
Broiled fish, biblical style
- 2 pounds fresh or defrosted fish
- Salt
- 4 cloves garlic, chopped
- Olive oil

- Red wine vinegar or lemon juice
- Lettuce
- Greek olives

Clean, rinse, and salt the fish. Rub with garlic, and brush with oil.

Preheat the broiler. Place the fish in an oiled pan. Broil small fish about 3 inches from the flame, larger fish about 5 inches away. Broil split fish skin side down. During the cooking, baste generously with olive oil and a little vinegar or lemon juice. The lemon juice is less authentic to Bible times than the vinegar. Lemons were rare and expensive at the time of Christ and the juice of sour grapes or other sour fruit or vinegar provided tartness where this was desired.

Serve the broiled fish on a bed of lettuce, garnished by Greek olives.

U

UPSIDE DOWN

Purpose
To become familiar with symbols attributed to Peter and to depict them using a paper mosaic technique.

Preparation
- Pictures of early Christian or contemporary mosaics
- Patterns for symbols representing Peter
- Construction paper
- Scissors
- Glue and brushes or glue sticks
- Pencils
- Rulers
- Toothpicks or hat pins
- Shallow trays
- Colorful magazine pages or other papers
- Envelopes
- Bibles

Procedure
Each of the twelve disciples was represented by visual symbols that indicated how they lived or died. A traditional symbol for Peter is the upside-down cross. Records of early Christian history tell us that Peter, at his own wish, was crucified with his head downward on an inverted cross. He did not feel worthy to be executed in the same manner as Jesus.

In addition to the cross, there are Scriptural references to images associated with Peter's life:

- Fish — Mark 1:16–18
- Rooster — Matthew 26:69–75
- Rock — Matthew 16:15–19
- Keys — Matthew 16:15–19
- Sheep — John 21:15–19

A number of early Christian images and symbols are represented in mosaics, an art form using small pieces of glass, ceramic, or stones anchored in mortar or plaster. The small pieces, called *tesserae*, fit together to form a picture. Mosaics appear in ancient buildings as decorations for walls, ceilings, and floors, as well as embellishments for courtyards and exterior walls. Look at pictures of early or modern mosaics to gain more information.

Assemble a paper mosaic type of collage to depict Peter's upside-down cross; then add simple cutouts of other symbols associated with his life to the background to complete the picture. Another plan would be to create each of the symbols using the paper mosaic technique.

Begin the paper mosaic process by first tracing or drawing the inverted cross onto a piece of light-colored construction paper, 9 inches square. With a pencil and a ruler mark sections 12 inches by 1/2 inch on a sheet of construction paper in a contrasting color. Cut the long strips, then snip 1/2-inch squares as needed.

Artists may share colors with each other. Cut textured and foil papers ahead of time and place in shallow trays for easy access.

Brush glue over a small area of the cross, then place paper bits close together on the glued surface. A toothpick or hat pin will make it easier to move paper squares into position. Continue until the cross shape is filled in with mosaic pieces. Choose 1/2-inch squares of a third color and follow the same procedure to fill in the background. Experiment with paper bits of different colors, sizes, and textures.

Check the Scripture references and choose some or all of the other symbols to add to the mosaic background. The additional symbols can be drawn and cut out, then glued in the areas surrounding the upside-down cross.

If each symbol will be illustrated with the mosaic method, draw the shape in the center of a square of paper and follow the process as described above. Finish the design by framing it with a border of pieces fit carefully around the edge of the background paper or with long strips of paper.

Add biblical references and titles to help observers identify the symbols. Display the finished art work so others can learn about the many facets of Peter's life. Arrange the collection of mosaic symbols as a border design along a wall or as a bulletin board composition.

V

VISION

Purpose
To create a banner to illustrate the visions of Cornelius and Peter.

Preparation
- Lengths of fabric (sailcloth, canvas, trigger) or sheets (twin bed size)
- Pencils
- Chalk
- Scrap paper
- Newspapers or plastic drop cloths
- Fabric paints
- Fabric markers
- Paint brushes
- Containers for water
- Bibles
- Reference books with pictures of clothing styles for centurions, slaves, and Bible-times people
- Overhead projector (optional)
- Acetate transparencies (optional)
- Transparency markers (optional)

Procedure
Acts chapter 10 records two important stories of visions—or dreams—sent by God to help people understand that the message of the Gospel is for the whole world. In Acts 10:3–6, Cornelius, a man who held an important position in the Roman army, had a vision in which he was instructed to send for the apostle Peter. In Acts 10:10–16, Peter had a vision in which he was ordered to minister to Cornelius. Although Cornelius believed in God, he did not know Jesus. When Peter went to Cornelius's house he told the Roman official, as well as his family and friends, about the wonderful things that Jesus said and did. Peter also told them that Jesus died and that God raised Jesus from the dead so that those who believe in Jesus could be saved. Peter explained that he had seen the risen Jesus. Cornelius and his family believed and were baptized. As a result of God's messages through the visions, God confirmed that the Gospel is for all people.

Read the accounts of the visions (Acts 10) and of the Old Testament information on clean and unclean animals (Leviticus 11). Make a banner, or a series of smaller fabric hangings, to illustrate the Scripture passages. A large sheet can become a mural with events placed in sequential order. Or, individual banners could feature various parts of the visions: Cornelius in centurion's uniform; angel appearing to Cornelius; soldier and slaves journey to Peter's home in Joppa; Peter on the roof praying; Peter's vision of unclean animals; Cornelius's men with Peter; the Gentiles hearing the Gospel.

Begin the project by planning the sketches on scrap paper. With pencil or chalk, draw a larger version on the fabric. For an easier transfer, see the instructions for using an overhead projector [O: Overhead Projector] to enlarge images.

Protect the work surface with newspapers or a drop cloth. Before painting, smooth out the fabric on the work surface. Hold the fabric securely in place by setting books or other heavy objects on the corners.

Paint the figures and background scenes, then allow to dry. Add details with a small paintbrush or fabric markers.

Fasten the finished banners to a wall or hang panels from rods.

Use the illustrations to explain the visions of Cornelius and Peter. For a dramatic presentation of the story, make processional banners! Create a panel for each part of the vision story. As the storyteller or narrator reads the Bible account, a new panel is exhibited. Banner bearers can remain holding the panel or can place the banner in a stand.

W

WITNESS

Purpose
To experience and report the Transfiguration story with fresh understanding by designing a newspaper.

Preparation
- Bible
- Sample newspaper
- Paper
- Pencils or pens
- Newsprint or poster board
- Tape or glue
- Scissors
- Computer equipment (optional)

Procedure
Peter was among the "inner circle" of Jesus' disciples. As one of Jesus' closest friends, he experienced meaningful moments with Jesus that he later shared with other disciples and, through Scripture, with us. One of these special moments occurred on the Mount of Transfiguration when Jesus was changed as the disciples' watched, and they saw Him glow in indescribable light and talk with Moses and Elijah. Peter's experience on the Mount of Transfiguration made him an eyewitness of Jesus' glory even before the Crucifixion and Resurrection. Like the Israelites in the desert, he experienced the mysterious cloud and the awesome voice of God. However, Jesus made this experience "top secret." Peter, James, and John were instructed to tell no one what had happened until after the Resurrection. Only then was Peter able to tell what he had seen (2 Peter 1:16–18). This kind of "first person" point of view is what a good reporter must have. Use this journalistic angle to teach the events of the Transfiguration and to help students uncover for themselves the meaning behind this remarkable story.

Read the story of the Transfiguration and discuss and/or role play the events. Invite the group to imagine that they are to be the ones who get to "break the story" to the world of what happened on the Mount of Transfiguration.

Prepare the "reporters" by observing and brainstorming what special approaches are needed to produce a newspaper. Begin by looking at a newspaper, preferably one that is responding to a major news event. Look at the layout of headlines, size of type, and arrangement of articles on the page. Notice any special boxes with condensed information and "bullets" of important ideas. Explain the factual five Ws—who, what, when, where, why—of front page news. Then look at the editorial page and discuss the difference between fact and opinion. Look at other features of the newspaper, including weather information, comics, advice columns, human interest stories, advertisements, and any other common characteristics of journalism to which learners seem attracted.

Using the paper as a model, brainstorm a list of articles and information that might be included. Be sure to cover such categories as the front page lead, the facts of the Transfiguration story; the human-interest angle, an interview with Peter; editorials backing the "new" church of Jesus Christ and maybe an opposing skeptical viewpoint; some related background stories of who Jesus was, His teachings, and what happened to Him; a cartoon strip, perhaps illustrating Peter's rambling about building booths; the weather and other incidentals, like ads for "rent-a-camel."

The production and style of the newspaper depends on resources available. Most simply, individual "journalists" can provide an article and "layout" can take place on poster board, newsprint, or the classroom wall. If word processing or computer design is possible, each person can help construct the "edition," or articles and information can be compiled and put together by one or a few skilled workers. If possible, publish and distribute the newspaper. Consider printing some or all of the articles in the church newsletter.

X

"X"

Purpose
To use a map activity to identify locations related to Peter's life and ministry.

Preparation
- Bibles
- Bible atlases and maps
- Basic map outline
- Pencils
- Paper
- Duplicating equipment
- Fine point markers
- Information about symbols representing Peter (See "U")
- Purchased stickers with Peter's symbols or self-made stickers, using small mailing labels

Advance Preparation
- Duplicate map.

Procedure
"X" marks the spot! One way to learn about the life of Peter is to use Scripture to help identify the places where he lived, worked, and traveled, and to transfer the information to a map to trace his ministry.

Distribute a blank map to each participant together with a list of Scripture references related to the places and passages that help trace the story of Peter's life. Provide pencils, Bibles, and reference materials, too. Instruct the group to look up each Scripture reference, to read about the place mentioned, and to find the location in a Bible atlas. Then pencil in the name of each place Peter visited on the blank map.

Once all of the places have been recorded on the map, make up symbols or use traditional images to design identification stickers. Color a symbol, such as a fish for Capernaum, and draw an "X" to mark the spot. Place the sticker as close to the place as possible. Be careful not to cover up other important sites.

When all of the places have been accurately tagged, refer to an atlas that indicates the paths taken by Peter; then draw a line tracing his journeys. Pause at each "X" to see if you recall what happened at the spot! Tell someone else about Peter's travels.

——— "X" MARKS THE SPOT ———

Peter's Places and Passages
- Galilee
  Matthew 4:18–20—Peter is called to follow Jesus

- Capernaum
  Matthew 8:14–17—Jesus heals Peter's mother-in-law

- Caesarea Phillipi
  Matthew 16:13–19—Peter's great confession
  Matthew 17—Peter witnesses Transfiguration

- Jerusalem
  John 12:12–19—Peter attends Triumphal Entry
  John 13:1–11—Peter attends Last Supper

- Sea of Tiberius
  John 21:1–14—Peter eats breakfast with Jesus

- Bethany
  Luke 24:50–53—Peter observes Ascension

- Jerusalem
  Acts 2:1–41—Peter is empowered by the Holy Spirit

- Joppa
  Acts 9:36–43—Peter heals Dorcas

- Jerusalem (Joppa)
  Acts 11:1–18—Peter converts Cornelius, the centurion

- Syria, Greece & Rome
  Tradition states Peter spread the Gospel in these places

PETER: Ideas A–Z Series

Y

YOU

Purpose
To consider the question Jesus placed before Peter— "Who do YOU say that I am?"—and to use story stems to offer personal answers.

Preparation
- "Story Stems"
- Duplicating equipment (or chalkboard and chalk or newsprint and markers)
- Pencils or pens
- Paper
- Bibles

Advance Preparation
- Duplicate a "Story Stems" sheet for each participant or write the phrases on a chalkboard or newsprint.

Procedure
Jesus gathered the disciples together for a variety of reasons—sometimes to teach or correct, sometimes to watch and pray, other times to celebrate and relax. But once, Jesus gathered the disciples to ask a very important question, "Who do YOU say that I am?" Peter was the star pupil, the first one to phrase the correct answer. Knowing the correct answer—"You are the Christ, the Son of the Living God"—and applying that information to life can be very different experiences, as Peter quickly discovered.

Each of us must answer the question Jesus put to the first disciples, "Who do YOU say that I am?" If we echo Peter's answer, then we must figure out what that means in our lives.

Use the following "Story Stems" as discussion starters or for private meditation as a way to help each participant acknowledge what Jesus as Son of the Living God means to them personally. If the "Story Stems" are used as a class activity refer to the phrases pre-written on a chalkboard or newsprint. Provide paper, pencils or pens, and Bibles and guide the group as they complete their responses. As an alternative, individual "Story Stem" sheets may be distributed and completed in class or at home.

If you say that Jesus is truly the Christ, the Son of the Living God . . .

. . . when did you discover the truth that Jesus is your Savior?

. . . how did you come to know Jesus as Son of God? Suddenly? Over a period of years?

. . . who helped you acknowledge Jesus' place in your life?

. . . how does this knowledge help you

- be a better person? friend? parent? son or daughter? sibling?

- face disappointments and failures?

- take risks?

- share your faith with others?

- live more abundantly?

. . . can others learn this truth by observing your life of faith?

. . . what part of your life are you still trying to control?

. . . what changes need to be made for Jesus to be truly Lord of your life?

Z

ZEBEDEE

Purpose
To introduce Zebedee, to explain about the life of a fisherman, and to reinforce learning with fish-related activities.

Preparation
Materials will be different for each activity.

Procedure
Zebedee was the father of the two disciples, James and John. Zebedee and his sons were fishing partners with Peter and his brother, Andrew. Peter and Andrew grew up in the town of Bethsaida and later lived in Capernaum, where Zebedee's fishing business was based. The partners fished in the Sea of Galilee, which is the larger of two freshwater lakes on the Jordan River. Fishing entailed plenty of hard work. The fishermen would work at night or start very early in the morning. The process of fishing consisted of casting nets, gathering them in, and then hauling the loaded nets into the boat. This was repeated until the boat was heavy with fish. Other important work for fishermen included repairing nets and keeping boats in good condition.

Fish was a major source of food for the people in the surrounding villages. One of the most plentiful species of fish caught in biblical times and still a principal catch today is the tilapia, also known as "Saint Peter's fish."

A great deal of Jesus' ministry encompassed the area around the Sea of Galilee. Many of the disciples were fishermen, which accounts for the emphasis on fishing terms and references. Jesus challenged the disciples to follow Him and to become "fishers of people."

Have some fun creating art or playing games with a fish theme. Use finished art projects to enhance the learning space!

—— **FISH PRINTS** ——

Preparation
- Freshly caught fish that is rather flat (perch, bluegill, or sunfish—keep refrigerated!)
- Tempera paints
- Paintbrushes
- Paper towels
- Newspapers
- Absorbent, thin paper such as newsprint
- Clean up supplies
- Refrigerator
- Clothesline
- Clip clothespins

Procedure

Place fish on newspaper and pat it dry with paper towels. Paint the fish from head to tail and gently press absorbent paper on painted surface of the fish. Rub fingers over fish to work the paint into the absorbent paper. Carefully lift one corner and peek to see if paint has transferred from the fish to the paper.

Remove print by peeling off slowly, then set aside to dry. Sometimes the first print has too much paint and will not show all of the details. Try several prints before painting the fish again.

When the prints are finished, wash the fish in cold water. Put it in a covered container and place in the refrigerator until the next person is ready to print.

Display the day's "catch" by clipping everyone's prints along a clothesline. Create a fish market that would impress Zebedee!

—— POP-UP PUPPET ——

Preparation

- Styrofoam cups
- Drinking straws
- Construction paper
- Pencils
- Scissors
- Glue
- Tape
- Permanent markers
- Blue plastic wrap, cellophane, or tissue paper
- Magazines, greeting cards, or fish stickers
- Stapler and staples
- Plastic netting from fruit or vegetable bags

Procedure

Fit blue plastic wrap, cellophane, or tissue inside of a cup and glue into place. Make small fish in any one of a number of ways: draw with markers then cut out; construct fish from colored paper; cut fish illustrations from magazines or greeting cards; use stickers. Fasten fish to the tops of two or three drinking straws, then punch the opposite end through the bottom of the cup.

Draw a boat with a sail or cut pieces from construction paper to represent a fishing boat. Attach the boat to the cup's top edge. Staple a small piece of net over one end of the boat. Use permanent markers to add waves and other sea life around the outside of the cup. Move the fish puppets up and down in the tiny "cup theater" sea.

—— FISH KITE OR WINDSOCK ——

Preparation

- Sheets of crepe paper or tissue paper
- Pencils
- Scissors
- Glue
- Miscellaneous papers
- Markers
- Tape
- String
- Hole punch

- Pipe cleaners or heavy wire
- Large, simple fish pattern

Procedure

Fashion a fish kite or windsock of brightly colored paper. Cut two large paper rectangles the same size. Trace the fish pattern on one of the sheets of paper. Stack the two papers and, following the pencil outline, cut both pieces to match. Squeeze a thin line of glue on the edges of one of the fish. Do not put glue on the tail and mouth areas. Place the second fish shape over the glued piece taking care to line up the edges.

Use markers to draw eyes, scales, and lines for the tail. Be sure to draw the details on both sides of the fish. Dots, zig-zags, and stripes will add more interest and color.

Form the wire or pipe cleaner into a circle large enough to fit snugly inside the fish's mouth. Slip the circle into the mouth opening so there is paper extending beyond the wire. Apply glue to the inside edge along the wire. Fold the edge of the paper over the wire onto the glue and press firmly. Allow to dry.

To strengthen the covered wire, reinforce with tape. Punch two holes in the taped area, on either side of the fish's mouth. Tie on strings to use as a handle or hanger.

Run out-of-doors or in a large play space and watch the fish sail in the air. For a festive touch, hang the fish overhead to swing in the breeze.

RESOURCES

Adult

Brown, Raymond E. with Karl P. Donfried and John Reumann. *Peter in the New Testament.* Minneapolis: Augsburg, 1973.

Filson, Floyd V. "Peter" in *The Interpreter's Dictionary of the Bible.* Nashville: Abingdon, 1962.

Koester, Nancy. *Simon Peter.* Minneapolis: Augsburg, 1984.

O'Connor, D. W. *Peter in Rome: The Literary, Liturgical and Archaeological Evidence.* New York: Columbia University Press, 1969.

Pittenger, W. Norman. *The Life of St. Peter.* Danbury, Conn.: Franklin Watts, 1971.

Sullender, R. Scott. *Peter: A Journey in Faith.* Prescott, Ariz.: Educational Ministries, Inc., 1986.

Walsh, William Thomas. *St. Peter the Apostle.* New York, N.Y.: Doubleday (Image), 1948.

Also: Numerous commentaries and reference books.

Youth

McElroy, Molly. *Jesus Forgives Peter.* St. Louis, Mo.: Concordia, 1985.

Mills, Peter. *Jailbreak.* Sisters, Oreg.: Questar, 1995.

Sanders, Nancy I. *Jesus Walks on Water.* St. Louis, Mo.: Concordia, 1995.

Storr, Catherine. *St. Peter and St. Paul.* Milwaukee, Wis.: Raintree Childrens Books, 1985.

Ulmer, Louise. *Jesus' 12 Disciples.* St. Louis, Mo.: Concordia, 1982.

Wezeman, Phyllis Vos and Judith Harris Chase. *Disciple Then! Disciples Now!* Prescott, Ariz: Educational Ministries, Inc., 1996.

Wezeman, Phyllis Vos, Anna L. Liechty, and Judith Harris Chase. *Pilgrimage: Seeking the Kingdom of God.* (An experiential curriculum for vacation Bible school and other Christian education settings, Mishawaka, Ind.: Active Learning Associates, Inc., 1998.)

Wezeman, Phyllis Vos and Colleen Aalsburg Wiessner. *Seaside with the Savior.* Elgin, Ill.: David C. Cook Publishing, 1995.

Also: Many children's Bibles and Bible storybooks.

Videos

Acts. Cokesbury, 1990.

"Apostles and Early Church." *Children's Heroes of the Bible.* Lutheran Church in America, 1988.

Easter. Christian Broadcasting Network, 1982.

"Easter Story." *Greatest Adventure: Stories from the Bible,* 1986.

Gospel of Mark. Cokesbury, 1988.

In Remembrance. Evangelical Films, 1979.

Jesus. Genesis Project, 1979.

Jesus Christ. Graded Press, 1985.

"Jesus Teaches and Calls Disciples." *Children's Heroes of the Bible.* Lutheran Church in America, 1988.

Luke. Cokesbury, 1991.

"Luke I," "Luke II," Luke III," Luke IV." *New Media Bible.* Genesis Project, 1975.

"Miracles of Jesus, The." *Animated Stories from the Bible.* Family Entertainment Network, 1987.